PRAISE FOR
THE 5 WEEK LEADERSHIP C...

"*The 5 Week Leadership Challenge* will spur you into action and help you write your own leadership story. I hope every leader reads it and follows its advice."

—Patrick Lencioni, CEO,
The Table Group, and Bestselling Author of
The Five Dysfunctions of a Team and *The Advantage*

"Patrick offers us a blend of storybook, pep talk, leadership guide, and reflection journal. Each day offers a story filled with candor, humor, and insight. Be warned: you will have to resist reading ahead!" —Dolly Chugh,
Jacob B. Melnick Term Professor, NYU Stern School of Business,
and Author of *The Person You Mean to Be: How Good People Fight Bias*

"I have spent my career working with some of the best leaders in the world. I have seen what makes some excel, while others struggle. I'm confident that taking on Patrick's *5 Week Leadership Challenge* and applying his ideas in your life will make you a leader that people choose to follow." —Joel Peterson,
Former Chairman, JetBlue Airways; Founder, Peterson Partners;
and Professor, Stanford University Business School

"*The 5 Week Leadership Challenge* isn't just a leadership book. It's a self-development workshop great for both new and experienced leaders. If you want to improve your team's performance immediately, read this book." —Dorie Clark,
Author of *Reinventing You* and Executive Education Faculty,
Duke University Fuqua School of Business

"As a former US Army infantry officer and ranger, serving with Patrick and watching him lead others firsthand, and in my current role as CEO of Skullcandy—I embrace the importance of developing great leaders of character. Patrick's words will inspire and challenge you to take your leadership to the next level."

—Jason Hodell,
CEO, Skullcandy

"Having spent a lifetime working with the best leaders in the world, I'm convinced that the lessons in *The 5 Week Leadership Challenge* can help you to achieve positive, lasting change in your life." —Marshall Goldsmith, *New York Times* #1 Bestselling Author of *Triggers, Mojo*, and *What Got You Here Won't Get You There*

"Creating a great culture begins with having great leaders who foster an environment where everyone believes what they do matters. Patrick's daily challenges over five weeks help you to become such a leader. Students of leadership, *like you*, will love and study this book!" —Chester Elton, Bestselling Author of *The Carrot Principle, All In*, and *Leading With Gratitude*

"Patrick's storytelling abilities make this book engaging, but it's his pragmatic lessons that will transform how you lead yourself and others. I especially love 'Explore Passion' and 'Understand Relationships' because these two factors lead all kinds of leaders to true fulfillment at work, at home, and in our communities." —Paul L. Corona, MBA, EdD, Clinical Professor of Leadership, Kellogg School of Management at Northwestern University

"Creating a culture of true belonging, where people can embrace their full selves at work, requires exceptional leaders who embody the right behaviors, support authentic teamwork, and challenge individuals to exceed their own expectations of themselves. This book is designed to help you to become that very leader—and learn more about yourself in the process. As you commit to understanding and sharing your personal leadership story over the course of this book, you'll find others will follow you not because they feel obliged to but because they truly want to." —Jennifer Brown, Award-winning Entrepreneur, Speaker, Diversity and Inclusion Consultant, and Author of *How to Be an Inclusive Leader*

"Patrick is not just an excellent writer and teacher but a true leader himself. Readable, research-backed, and deeply relevant for this time, this book will give you the courage and clarity to lift yourself and others to whole new heights. If you want to take your leadership to the next level—read, dare, do." —Margie Warrell, PhD, Bestselling Author, Speaker, and CEO, Global Courage Leadership

"Nothing excites me more as an executive coach than helping leaders to reach their full potential. It's with that spirit that I unequivocally recommend that you read and put *The 5 Week Leadership Challenge* into practice. Allow Patrick's stories, lessons, and challenges to take you to new heights." —Eddie Turner, Executive Coach, International Bestselling Author, Facilitator, Speaker, Radio Host of *Keep Leading!*® Podcast

"*The 5 Week Leadership Challenge* is packed with immense substance on leadership while also being highly entertaining. Through Patrick's wealth of experience, he offers us insight into leadership principles through the way we learn best—stories. He then helps us apply these principles through pragmatic exercises that are meaningful enough to build our awareness and yet bite-sized enough to internalize. From my experience working with CEOs and senior leaders from places like LinkedIn to high-growth startups, this book hits the mark on how we can digest and apply the most important leadership principles in today's world."

—Prakash Raman,
formerly in Executive Development,
LinkedIn, and CEO, Raman Consulting

"Leading a large and complex business, I know firsthand the importance of having exceptional leaders at every level. If you aspire to lead others or are far along in your leadership journey, you would be smart to invest thirty-five days in yourself by reading and putting to use Patrick's lessons and insights."

—Howard Friedman,
President and CEO, Post Consumer Brands

"In a world of constant change, people are looking for leaders who can become a source of confidence and strength. *The 5 Week Leadership Challenge* helps you to be that type of leader. Patrick's insights will help you level up your current approach to leadership, starting with why you choose to lead, what you want to accomplish, and the legacy you want to leave." —Dr. Nadya Zhexembayeva, Scientist, Entrepreneur, and Author of *The Chief Reinvention Officer Handbook*

"Far too many leaders fail to find meaning and happiness in their lives and work because they don't tackle the tough questions about their motivations, strengths, and purpose. This book offers a step-by-step guide for you to work on yourself and the impact you want to make. Patrick is a first-class storyteller, candidly sharing his own leadership struggles and successes to guide readers through a real plan for becoming the leader they want to be."   —Karen Dillon,
Former Editor, *Harvard Business Review*, and *New York Times* Bestselling Coauthor of *How Will You Measure Your Life?*

"As a first-time CEO and company founder, I found Patrick's book to be something rare: a practical guide and a source of inspiration. The stories made me think deeply about how to be a better leader, while the checklists helped me set daily priorities. And as a longtime writer, I was moved by the engaging personal stories and lessons learned. *The 5 Week Leadership Challenge* has inspiration for everyone, whether you are a seasoned leader or an aspiring one."
—Julian Guthrie,
New York Times Bestselling Author of *The Billionaire and the Mechanic* and *How to Build a Spaceship*; Pulitzer Prize Nominee; CEO, Mindset Alpha; and CEO and Founder, Alphy

"As a global business leader, it's imperative to embrace the development of each team member, creating and enabling leaders across your organization. The importance of culture cannot be overstated, and integral to the fabric of any truly inclusive culture are the unique stories of each leader. Patrick's work embodies beautiful storytelling that encourages us to consider how to best capture our own story by reflecting on the diverse experiences of our lives with the objective of continuous learning and growth."   —Anne Chow, CEO, AT&T Business, and Coauthor of *The Leader's Guide to Unconscious Bias*

"*The 5 Week Leadership Challenge* is ideal for all of us in need of guidance on our leadership journey. Patrick teaches how pointed reflection, a deep understanding of one's own leadership values, and the ability to recognize when leadership is actually called for are practices available to anyone who wants to be a better leader."   —David A. Owens, PhD, PE,
Evans Family Executive Director of the Wond'ry, and Faculty at Vanderbilt University's Owen Graduate School of Management

THE
5 WEEK
LEADERSHIP
CHALLENGE

Thirty-Five Action Steps to Becoming the Leader You Were Meant to Be

Patrick Leddin, PhD

HarperCollins
LEADERSHIP

AN IMPRINT OF HARPERCOLLINS

NEW YORK

Published by HarperCollins Leadership, an imprint of HarperCollins Focus LLC.

Any internet addresses, phone numbers, or company or product information printed in this book are offered as a resource and are not intended in any way to be or to imply an endorsement by HarperCollins Leadership, nor does HarperCollins Leadership vouch for the existence, content, or services of these sites, phone numbers, companies, or products beyond the life of this book.

ISBN 978-1-4002-2531-6 (eBook)
ISBN 978-1-4002-2530-9 (HC)
ISBN 978-1-4002-2533-0 (TP)

Library of Congress Control Number: 2021933391

Printed in the United States of America
22 23 24 25 26 LSC 10 9 8 7 6 5 4 3 2 1

Thank you to my wife, Jamie, who encourages me to see the potential within myself and to our family, Clay, Alex, and Kevin, for whom I hope to achieve that potential. To my extended family, friends, and colleagues, I am forever grateful for lessons taught, insights shared, and examples provided.

Lastly, to leaders who earnestly strive to become better versions of themselves, I hope that the contents of this book will help you to write your leadership story.

CONTENTS

FOREWORD

There are some business books that you quickly skim over during a long flight and then never touch again.

This is not that book.

The 5 Week Leadership Challenge is truly a leadership workbook, which dares and inspires the reader to improve themselves throughout the journey. Patrick serves as an excellent guide; his stories capture your attention and welcome you into his family as he takes you through his personal leadership journey. We follow him on his adventure as he moves from jumping out of airplanes in the army to starting his own consulting firm and to finding his balance between work and his wonderful family.

The most amazing facet of the book is that real and powerful leadership lessons are woven gracefully into the stories. In one moment, you are following Patrick along as he hikes up Mount Kilimanjaro, and then suddenly you realize what the leadership lesson of the story is—just as Patrick brings it up. The result is a brilliant moment of serendipity in each chapter as you realize your own growth as Patrick learns along with you.

Throughout my extensive research on the value and impact of trust, I have seen time and time again the power of stories. Learning from the experiences of others allows us to feel their emotions, empathize with their highs and lows, and see just how our behaviors impact the lives of those around us. In fact, the very act of sharing one's own stories authentically lends itself to creating a high level of trust between the storyteller and the reader.

As you read through *The 5 Week Leadership Challenge*, you will undoubtedly be inspired by Patrick's level of transparency and continual desire to get better. I believe you'll also feel that Patrick not only understands you as a reader but that he trusts you, too—and, in turn, I believe that you'll be inspired to reciprocate that trust.

You will not only learn how Patrick has improved over the course of his career, but you, too, will be challenged to get better as a leader. Patrick is an innovative storyteller who openly welcomes you into his life and allows you to learn from both his failures and victories. He openly confronts reality and invites you to do the same. At the end of each chapter, Patrick provides you with challenging self-reflection questions and tasks, allowing you to apply the lessons to your life immediately while also ensuring a lifetime of value.

Don't rush through this book in a weekend—it's called *The 5 Week Leadership Challenge* for a reason. Instead, work through the book as it's intended, taking each chapter as a daily ritual to improve yourself as a leader. This way of learning is more of a process than a onetime event. The result will be not only greater learning but far greater application and impact in your life.

I am lucky enough to have known Patrick throughout most of the time period of the book. He has always innately understood the power of trust and how it truly is the one thing that changes everything.

I invite you to let the insights you'll glean from his wonderful book change you, too.

Stephen M. R. Covey
New York Times and # 1 *Wall Street Journal*
bestselling author of *The Speed of Trust* and
coauthor of *Smart Trust*
November 23, 2020

WELCOME
TO THE CHALLENGE

T he escalator ride from the first floor allowed me to better appreciate the impressive lobby in the downtown Beijing hotel. I knew the grand ballroom was located somewhere on the second level, but navigating the facility was proving a bit tricky, as was asking for directions, given my rudimentary understanding of Mandarin. Fortunately, the signage guided me to the correct room. I opened the door and was immediately taken aback by the sight of hundreds of chairs standing ready for the audience's arrival.

A few hotel employees were milling about in the front of the room conducting last-minute sound checks and adjusting the angle and clarity of the presentation projectors. They greeted me warmly and oriented me to the stage by showing me where to place my laptop, how to affix and operate the wireless microphone, and asking me what I needed to feel comfortable. In all honesty, feeling comfortable was not likely to happen. I asked for a glass of water in response to their hospitality and as a half-hearted attempt to calm the butterflies that were starting to take flight in my stomach. One person scurried off to find the water and the others went back to what they were doing prior to my arrival.

Taking a deep breath, I set out to settle my nerves by reviewing the agenda and mentally walking through my presentation. I knew my topic well, having recently delivered my message in cities throughout the United States and Europe, but there were a couple of aspects about today's situation that concerned me.

Prior to that week, I had never spoken to an audience in China, especially an audience consisting of several hundred businesspeople. I didn't want to speak too quickly or be lost in cultural translation. I felt that under normal conditions, I could overcome these hurdles, but what really concerned me was why people were coming that day. They weren't there to see me. I was essentially the opening act for a much bigger name who was going to take the stage as the session's main event. Let's face it, few people are excited to see the opening act.

Thinking about this reality, I pictured thousands of emails flying through Beijing cyberspace in the weeks leading up to the event, each inviting the recipient to attend a business conference in the grand ballroom of an iconic hotel to listen and learn from one of the greatest business minds of our time. The main speaker's name would then appear in large font followed by the names of his bestselling books. For many, that information alone would be enough to secure their attendance. Those who needed a bit more information or decided to read the entire message would eventually come to the words "and Dr. Patrick Leddin" in a much smaller, less grandiose typeface.

Now, don't get me wrong. I actually didn't mind being the lesser name on the day's agenda. In fact, I was honored to be there. I had respected the keynote speaker for years and personally looked forward to hearing him speak that day. What concerned me was the conversation I'd had with him the previous day when he arrived in town. Sitting in a small conference room, the two of us discussed the plan for the event. It was my understanding that I was to speak for approximately forty-five minutes about how to effectively lead yourself and others in today's world. He would then take the stage and speak for the remainder of the morning. The split made sense to me and likely aligned with the expectations of the crowd. However, he saw the session unfolding much differently.

"I'd prefer you speak for a bit over two hours and I will do about a thirty-minute talk with fifteen minutes for questions and answers," he said, adding that he thought my message would truly resonate with the audience. I was flattered by his kind words, but expressed concerns with audience expectations. I can't remember how the rest of the conversation played out other than him being amazingly convincing. At some point I agreed with his request. That night, I sat down at my computer to revise my presentation to adjust for my extended time slot. I added stories about my personal experience leading teams in the army, at a publicly traded company, and at my own startup. My intent was to use the stories as a means of conveying various principles of leadership through personal narratives. I knew that past audiences had found similar stories useful and I hoped that the next day's attendees would also.

I didn't sleep much that night; morning came quick and before I knew it the grand ballroom was filling with people. I was pacing a groove into the backstage carpet.

At the top of the hour, the host took the stage and greeted attendees in Mandarin. The crowd was energized by his words. As he finished his comments, he quickly transitioned into English, introduced me as the first speaker, and asked the audience to give me a warm welcome. I stepped onstage, shook his hand, and as the applause tapered off, I began my presentation. The next 120 minutes were a whirlwind as I spoke to the packed room about how to effectively lead yourself and others. I told them about my own experiences leading others. I shared what I did well and areas where I struggled. I also shared my observations of others doing the same.

Despite my misgivings, the audience's reaction was better than I had expected. When I took the stage, I was merely hoping to keep them engaged and share a few useful pieces of information to make their own leadership journey more successful, but as I wrapped up my two-hour presentation, it was clear that the room was engaged and genuinely interested in what I had to say. In fact, after the main speaker finished his presentation and opened the floor up for questions, I was called back onstage as many of the questions were for me.

Later that day, the main speaker and I were sitting in the back seat of a car heading across town. He turned to me and asked, "Where do you get all of your stories?"

His question that afternoon and the response of the audience that day convinced me that stories are powerful—especially when sharing a story helps someone to change their behavior, improve performance, or achieve what matters most to them. Stories play a large role in my Vanderbilt University classroom, helping students move from concept to practice. The leadership stories that you will read over the next five weeks will allow you to move closer each day to becoming the leader that you mean to be. There are thirty-five leadership stories, one for each day of the next five weeks, along with accompanying actions steps, questions for you to answer, and a small challenge.

The thirty-five days are grouped into five weeks, each with a distinct theme. In the first week—Gain Perspective—you will explore ten leadership mindsets. I start with these, because how you think about leading yourself and others will directly influence your actions and results. Understanding these mindsets and assessing your own thinking in each area will be key to your success.

In week two—Discover Purpose—you will work to uncover the reason why you choose to lead. By the end of the week, you will craft your leadership purpose statement. Leadership can be very rewarding, but it is also tough. Knowing why you lead will serve as a source of energy to draw from when times get tough—and they will get tough.

The third week is Determine Priorities, and the fourth week is Create Plans. In those weeks, you will have the opportunity to draft a few key priorities for yourself and the plans you will follow to move your priorities from thoughts to results.

The fifth and final week is Inspire Performance. You will explore how to perform at the highest level, both as an individual and as a leader of others.

HOW TO USE THIS BOOK

I wrote this book with the expectation that you would complete a lesson every day of the week, Sunday through Saturday. However, as I've shared the 5 Week Leadership Challenge with other people, I've seen that many people like to do them in four- or five-day increments each week. (Appendix A provides you sample schedules that you can follow.) In all honesty, I'm less concerned with the plan you create for yourself than I am that your plan is realistic and doable. Also, I've had people go through the 5 Week Leadership Challenge with other leaders, acting as accountability partners to one another. They do the daily reading on their own, but get together weekly to discuss progress. That can be very powerful. If you choose to work through the content with other leaders, I've created a plan that you can follow in Appendix B.

Each daily challenge has space below it where you should take notes and write down your thoughts. Use this book as a journal that you can revisit time and again. You'll get the best results by dedicating fifteen to twenty minutes each day to the 5 Week Leadership Challenge.

One last thing before we start. If you find yourself asking the same question that the keynote speaker asked me when we were China—where all of my stories come from—they come from my time as an officer in the army, a project manager at KPMG Consulting, a senior consultant at FranklinCovey, and the owner of two businesses, Wedgewood Consulting Group and Leddin Group. They stem from my time as a professor at Vanderbilt University and from the extensive traveling that I've done for work and fun. Most importantly, they derive from nearly thirty years of marriage to my spouse, Jamie, raising two amazing kids, Alex and Clay, and working with a wide range of team members, leaders, and friends.

Enjoy the journey.

Patrick

GAIN
PERSPECTIVE

What did I get myself into?

That was the question that kept running through my mind. I was thirty-four years old and married with two children. The business my spouse, Jamie, and I had started a few years earlier was rapidly growing with offices in three states, an amazing team of employees, and an increasing list of clients. The daily demands of work and home were abundant. Yet after much discussion, research, and reflection, I had decided, with the full support of my team, clients, and—most importantly—family, to sell our house, move from Florida to Kentucky, and pursue my doctorate at the University of Kentucky. I knew it would be five years of schoolwork, while running our business and using what little time wasn't consumed by the first two demands to maintain my personal relationships.

The acceptance letter had arrived a few months earlier. We sold our home, said goodbye to our friends, drove to our new town, and moved into a hotel waiting for our new house in Louisville to be ready. It had been an exciting adventure. Now the excitement was in the rearview mirror and I was dealing with the reality of being back in school. I sat down in a coffee shop across the street from my hotel with a coffee in one hand and the details of my first homework assignment in the other. It was clear that I was going to be working into the wee hours of the morning. I read the first paragraph of the assigned reading three times. After the third pass, I still didn't understand what the author was saying. She was using language that was all foreign to me. It was English, but it was written for academics and I read business articles. Clearly, this wasn't going well. I felt in over my head and I wasn't sure what to do about it.

That night, I went back to our hotel room. As I climbed into bed, Jamie whispered in the darkness, "How'd the studying go?"

I responded, "I think I made a big mistake. Maybe we shouldn't have done this."

Fortunately, her face was hidden in the shadows of the dark room, so I was unable to see her nonverbal response. Years later, she informed me that her initial reaction was shock and concern. But her words conveyed something else. In that moment, Jamie said exactly what I needed. She calmly said, "Let's just take it one day, one work meeting, and one class session at a time. You are going to make it through the program. Plus, no matter how hard it gets, let's promise to make no decisions until the end of each semester."

Her answer was brilliant. Why? Because she put everything in perspective. While my mind was racing to all that I had before me, she reassured me and told me to calm down. She didn't say that it wouldn't be tough; she just counseled me to take it as it comes and not to borrow trouble. Jamie reminded me that when you are in the throes of the day-to-day, you can lose perspective, allow your emotions to drive decisions, and do something you will later regret.

Five years later, I graduated. Our business was still growing. My relationships were still intact.

Perspective matters.

It especially matters for you as a leader.

It is through the lens of perspective that you determine what is important, choose your behaviors, meet the needs of those you serve, and deliver meaningful results. Arguably, everything that you do as a leader flows from your mindset, and spending time to gain perspective is critical to successful leadership. That's why the first week of the 5 Week Leadership Challenge focuses on perspective. Perspective allows you to better understand why you choose to lead in the first place, how to think about leading others, and where to put your best energy.

Over the course of the first week, you will explore ten leadership mindsets. Are these the only mindsets? No. However, they are ten of the most critical, and each requires your time, energy, and best thinking. By the end of the week, you will be able to assess yourself against each of the ten mindsets and develop concrete steps to better understand what it means to accomplish goals with and through others.

If you are just starting to lead others, this will be a rare opportunity to consider what it means to think like a leader and to assess your willingness to embrace these mindsets. If you are bit further in your leadership journey, this is a chance to take stock of your progress to date and determine if some of your thinking is leading you astray. For all of us, it's a rare time to step back, assess where we stand, and gain fresh perspectives to help us to more effectively lead others.

DAY 1

CLARIFY FOCUS

Many years ago, I was a paratrooper in the United States Army's 82nd Airborne Division. I was paid to jump out of perfectly good airplanes. My first nighttime jump took place at 2:00 a.m. in the skies above Fort Stewart, Georgia. That night, some 1,500 paratroopers jumped from twenty-two airplanes cruising at 800 feet (243 meters) above swamps and pine trees.

I found nighttime parachute jumps to be particularly exciting. The standard practices of preparing to exit the aircraft came with an extra bit of exhilaration. When the jump doors opened, the glow of sunlight that entered the cabin during daytime operations wasn't present, leaving everyone to rely on the glow of the green "go" light to guide much of their movement to the exit. Additionally, the ever-present roaring winds and booming engines that filled your ears during every jump were accompanied at night by the enthusiastic shouts of your fellow troopers yearning to get out the door. Something about nighttime jumps made everyone more eager and you could hear it in their shouts. It was an assault on your senses. Then, after clearing the airplane door and looking up to check your parachute, all of the sound goes away. In a matter of seconds you go from crammed on the plane with an excited group of fellow paratroopers to floating in solitude through the stillness of the night.

On that summer night of my first nighttime jump, I went through the standard procedure of ensuring my parachute was in working order and checking to see if any fellow jumpers were too close. All looked good with the parachute and, although I could see other parachutes floating around me, none were near enough to raise concerns.

All seemed fine, until I realized it wasn't.

As I peered toward the approaching ground, I saw a dark patch of trees a few hundred feet below my feet. Way off to the left was a much lighter area produced by the soft sands of the drop zone. The problem was that I was moving further into the dark area with no chance of avoiding it. Unlike parachutes used in many other scenarios, the ones used in large airborne operations afford the jumper little ability to steer or change direction. It makes sense under these conditions because you don't want to have 1,500 people with steerable parachutes going every which way in the night sky. That is a recipe for an in-air collision. That said, I would have appreciated something a bit more maneuverable that night. As I approached the trees, I braced for impact knowing I had no choice but to plow into inevitable danger. I raised my arms in front of my face, put my knees together, tucked my chin, and hoped for the best.

In this situation, I was a prisoner of circumstance. I couldn't control where the planes flew, when I jumped out the door (the plane's green light and fellow troops pushing from behind saw to that), the strength of the prevailing winds, or the type of parachute I was using.

Over the past twenty-five-plus years, I've worked with individuals, teams, and organizations who suggest they, too, are at the mercy of bad work situations and have little or no control over their careers. Nothing could be further from the truth. It's true that we can't control everything, nor should we try. However, we have far more choices available to us than we usually believe exist if we simply choose to lead ourselves.

Let's face it—things aren't always going to go well. Sometimes you will land in the trees. Your trees probably aren't hundred-foot Georgia pines that get in your way, but they can be organizational processes that annoy you, IT systems that are overly cumbersome, a person whose behavior is upsetting, or many other sources of concern. These trees seem to pop up whenever you try to lead others to accomplish goals that matter. You can't avoid every problem, but you can learn from each setback, brush yourself off, and get back on track as quickly as possible. You can also learn to focus your energies on what you can do in the moment.

If you don't like the results you are currently achieving, do something about it. If you are disappointed in your team's performance, step up and help out. If you are unhappy with your choice of career, don't settle. Take a positive step in the right direction—today! Time is ticking. Your parachute is much more steerable than you think. Choose to avoid the trees and accomplish what matters most to you, to those you lead, and to those you care for the most.

As I hung from the limbs of the trees by my parachute harness, I couldn't see my hand in front of my face in the pressing darkness. My training taught me that I could deploy my reserve parachute and climb down. I decided to go that route, but first I wanted to see how secure I was in the tree. I tugged on my parachute risers and slipped a few inches. Suddenly, I found myself standing safely on the ground. Although I assumed I was high up in the tree, I was only six inches from the ground. It was my only jump in the army where I landed on both feet.

My takeaway from that jump is to always be willing to take a calculated risk, focus on what you can control, and go for it. You might be surprised when you land on your feet.

DAY 1: CLARIFY FOCUS

Today's Thought

You may not be able to move the trees, but you can choose how to deal with them.

Today's Questions

1.   What trees tend to occupy too much of your time and energy?

   _____

   _____

2.   What trees do you see in the work lives of your team members that are occupying too much of their time and energy?

   _____

   _____

3.   How might you remove some of those trees?

   _____

   _____

Today's Challenge

Pick one of the trees that you listed above that is occupying too much time and energy in your life and let it go. Don't talk about it. Don't think about it. Just let it go.

DAY 2

ENGAGE PEOPLE

T here is a couch in our house that carries special meaning for Jamie and me. On that very couch in the summer of 2001, we made a bold decision. At the time, Jamie and I both had full-time jobs and the responsibility of raising our children together. Earlier that year, a former business associate of mine had asked me to assist his organization in its effort to identify a graduate study program for their high potential employees. Essentially, they wanted to send approximately thirty employees per year to a master's program at the organization's cost. The problem was twofold. First, there were a lot of stakeholders involved in the decision, each with a different idea of which university to partner with and how to go about selecting which employees to send to the program. Second, they were in need of someone who could assess universities, conduct phone interviews with faculty and staff to determine the best fit, and visit a short list of institutions leading up to a recommended course of action. Although I appreciated our friend's inquiry, the timing didn't feel quite right. So, I passed on the opportunity. Jamie decided otherwise, and one day in the spring of 2001, she called our friend and said that she could help him with the project. That night, when I came home after work, she informed me that she would be starting the project the following week.

She made the right choice.

The effort lasted about three months and it went extremely well. Jamie and I worked our normal jobs during the day, and at night I would help her with the project. By midsummer, she had visited multiple universities and presented our recommendations to the client. They agreed with everything she proposed. Then, they asked if we would help them implement the program. Flattered by the request and eager to see the recommendations put into action, we had a decision to make. On one hand, the project was fun and allowed us to stretch ourselves. We also realized how well we enjoyed working together. On the other hand, we both had day jobs with benefits and security. Two days later, we were sitting on the couch assessing our choices. In that moment, we elected to quit our jobs and start our own company, Wedgewood Consulting Group. At the time, it was a group of two people (Jamie and me) who lived on a street called Wedgewood Drive. Eleven years later, we had locations in three states, a growing team of amazing people, an enviable client list, and a position on *Inc.* magazine's list of the fastest-growing privately held businesses in the United States.

Things were going very well. Then, it happened.

Someone offered to buy our business. The interest came out of nowhere. In 2011, I was working on a project in Europe and Asia for the better part of three months. Our daughter, Alex, had recently started college and our then-thirteen-year-old son, Clay, was in eighth grade. We managed to work out our schedules so that Clay and Jamie could go along with me on the extended business trip, thinking that we would make an adventure out of it.

We returned in mid-December and shortly afterward, I received a phone call from my former manager at KPMG Consulting. (I had worked at KPMG just after leaving the army and I often chatted with my former colleagues.) My prior manager had left KPMG as well and he was catching me up on his career. I mentioned that we had been out of the country on a project. He inquired about our clients and our team, asking how things had gone in our absence. I told him that everything went well. We had built a great team of employees who worked well together and did an exceptional job supporting our clients. I wasn't exaggerating. They were terrific people and they did excellent work. After providing him with an update, he asked me if I'd like to talk to his boss, because they were looking to acquire a couple of companies in an effort to expand their offerings and we seemed to be a great fit. I agreed to a call. After I hung up the phone, I told Jamie the news.

The next week was a blur as we talked to the prospective buyer, learned more details about his interest, expressed our concerns about what would happen to Wedgewood employees post-sale, and began to construct the framework of a deal. Things were moving quickly and it was thrilling. To some extent, every entrepreneur dreams of building a business, launching a product, or creating a service that others value. If you have ever sold a business, however, you know that a great amount of effort goes into closing the deal.

We hired legal and financial advisors to help us navigate the intricacies of the sale, to determine what the firm was worth, and to manage the complexity of the transaction. We also engaged with business consultants to address employee and client communication. At one point, it seemed like we had someone doing something for us on every front.

Then, things slowed down—way down. Every issue became a point of contention. Quick decisions turned into a series of conference calls all seemingly focused on one thing: money. The transaction we were working to strike started to unravel.

Somewhere along the way, we had lost sight of what the sale of the business was really all about. Yes, money mattered. I won't lie about that. However, we had entered the situation seeing the sale not as a onetime transaction, but as an opportunity to transform Wedgewood Consulting Group into something new. The company acquiring us was bigger, growing fast, and able to offer our people more career opportunities. Jamie and I were convinced that the sale was a good move for all involved. It was about the organization's transformation. It was about our team members and what would happen to them after the sale closed. It was about our clients and honoring the commitments we had made to them over the years. It was about the buyers and what terms would work for them. And, it was about us and how we would handle honoring all of those relationships.

One evening, Jamie and I picked up the phone and called the potential buyer. We hadn't talked directly to him in weeks as the attorneys, accountants, and consultants had been doing much of the speaking for us. We shared our concerns about the purchase with him and our desire to give our employees as smooth of a transition as possible. He shared how much they could afford to pay for our company and how he intended to integrate our team into his company's culture. In that moment, we struck a deal.

That's the power of real people talking to real people about real people. The attorneys, accountants, and consultants all had their roles to play, but as leaders, we had to ensure that the people were kept at the center of the discussion. Never forget that, as a leader, you need to keep people at the forefront of your decisions. Getting things done with and through others is the essence of leadership.

DAY 2: ENGAGE PEOPLE

Today's Thought

Leading people is not about transactions. Leading people is about transformation.

Today's Questions

1. When you are working with others, whose agenda are you on—your agenda, their agenda, or a shared agenda?

    _____

    _____

2. Do you overly focus on the task at hand and forget that people are involved?

    _____

    _____

3. What might you do to strike a better balance between people and tasks?

    _____

    _____

Today's Challenge

Pick one relationship that has become overly transactional and take a step today toward bringing the human dimension back into the relationship.

RETHINK FAILURE

L ucy Westlake is impressive. She's an amazing runner, triathlete, and mountain climber. *Outside* magazine called her "the grittiest thirteen-year-old mountain climber we know." Lucy also has a genuinely good heart and is committed to making a positive mark on the world. By all indications, she is well on her way to building an incredible legacy.

I have had the chance to share a few stages with Lucy. Together we have talked about leadership, facing challenges, and overcoming failure. At first blush, people might be surprised that a teenage girl and a fifty-year-old business professor, writer, and speaker are able to capture the attention of several hundred sales leaders, but it works.

Why?

Because we are all dealing with the same thing. We all set goals, we all work hard to accomplish them, and we all know what it feels like to win and what it feels like to fail.

What Lucy has figured out at a young age is how to keep failure in perspective. How?

A couple of years ago, Lucy and her dad set out to climb Denali in Alaska. Her aim was to make it to the top and claim the record as the youngest female to conquer the highest point in each of the fifty United States of America. Denali is the highest mountain peak in North America, with a summit elevation of 20,310 feet (6,191 meters) above sea level. It's a challenge.

After twenty days on the mountain, they had to descend. Weather made reaching the summit impossible. As a result, Lucy "failed" in a couple of ways:

1. She didn't summit Denali.
2. She didn't become the youngest female in history (at least not yet) to reach the highest point of all fifty states.

As you might imagine, Lucy was disappointed in the outcome. You would be, too. She had invested a ton of time, energy, emotion, and effort into reaching her goal. Every other climb had gone flawlessly.

But what she learned from failing is a victory.

Don't take my word for it. Listen to what Lucy told me when I asked her about what she learned from Mt. Denali.

"It took a lot of grit just to get up to the camp that we reached on Denali. It was one of the hardest things that I had ever done," she said. "It also took a lot of grit to accept that we didn't make it to the top. It was really disappointing, but I feel if I gave up then, I didn't accomplish what I could. I love mountain climbing by itself, but also I love the things that mountain climbing allows me to do. My gift of climbing mountains has the ability to inspire others to do what they want to do."

Here are three things we can all learn from Lucy's ability to fail gracefully:

1. TRUST IN OTHERS

Imagine for a moment that you are Lucy's dad, Rodney. You're her climbing partner and the two of you are working your way up a snow-covered mountain. At one point, the terrain gets a bit more technical and you decide to rope up for safety. You attach one end of a rope to her and the other end to you. If she starts to fall, she trusts you to catch her. If you start to fall, you must trust her to catch you.

No doubt, you are doing the math. Rodney has a significant weight advantage over his teenage daughter. What makes up for the mathematical delta? He has confidence in her and her abilities. He has watched her try, fail, try again, and succeed since she started hiking mountains at age seven. He knows that each successive failure and victory has made her stronger. In the early days of her hiking career, if he had chastised her for failures rather than coached her through them, she would undoubtedly see failure in a very different light. It would not have been something to learn from but something to be judged about. In turn, she would have played small, avoided risks, and likely quit trying altogether.

The same is true for you as a leader. You have to realize that how you react to failure matters. Failure is inevitable—your reaction is not.

2. DETERMINATION TO ACHIEVE GREATNESS

There is a long list of unknown poets, musicians, and other dreamers who gave up on achieving greatness at the first sign of failure. Instead of standing at the summit of their own success, they settled for something less. They decided that good was good enough.

Lucy could certainly do this. She already holds the title for the youngest female to reach the highest point in the lower forty-eight states. That's pretty darn good, but she is determined to do more. She is determined to achieve greatness.

As a leader, you will experience failure and disappointment. That's expected when you try new things and strive to be great at something. How you process that failure and how you develop others to deal with it is often the difference between settling and soaring.

3. RESILIENCE IN THE FACE OF FAILURE

When we get knocked down, some of us have a difficult time getting back up and trying again. Not only do we lose the drive to summit the mountain that beat us, but we decide that we are no longer a climber at all.

The poet puts down his pen.

The musician sets down her instrument.

The leader gives up.

The challenge is that you build resiliency when you don't need it. You invest in your mind, body, spirit, and relationships every day knowing that those investments will pay huge dividends in the future. They will give you a deep well of resiliency to draw from when failure comes. And it will come.

Lucy didn't stop after Denali. She continues to climb mountains, and has summited Russia's Mt. Elbrus (the highest point in Europe) and Pico de Orizaba (the highest point in Mexico). I have no doubt that Lucy will climb Mt. Denali and any other mountain she sets out to conquer in life. Her determination and resiliency will see to that. She has also inspired others. Since we started presenting together, I have summited Mt. Kilimanjaro, the highest point in Africa.

You will learn more about my Mt. Kilimanjaro hike and what it taught me on Day 7. In the meantime, let's explore your relationship with failure and how you process it.

DAY 3: RETHINK FAILURE

Today's Thought

If you want to accomplish something that you have never accomplished before, you will face setbacks and failure. It comes with the territory. Great leaders learn from failures and continue to move forward. Failure is inevitable. Your response to failure is your choice.

Today's Questions

1. Have past failures increased or diminished your determination for greatness?

   _____

   _____

2. What dreams have you given up on and settled for something less?

   _____

   _____

3. Have you been knocked down in the past and managed to get back up and try again?

   _____

   _____

4. How deep is your well of resiliency?

    _____

    _____

5. What are you doing right now to invest in your mind, relationships, body, and spirit?

    _____

    _____

Today's Challenge

Think about a recent failure that you've experienced. Identify one thing you can learn from that failure to help you to become a better leader.

DAY 4

FIND GUIDES

A couple of years ago, my son, Clay, and I set out to hike to the top of Mt. Sherman, roughly two hours outside of Denver, Colorado. The mountain's peak sits at 14,036 feet (4,278 meters) and offers breathtaking views in every direction. With an ascent of slightly over 2,000 feet (609.6 meters) and only a five-mile (eight-kilometer) round-trip trek from the parking lot, the summit was going to be challenging, but manageable.

However, this trip came with a twist. Winter came early that year.

When we arrived in the Denver area two days earlier, the weather was starting to turn bad. Snow was falling, the temperature was dropping, and the wind was picking up. We asked a couple of people their thoughts on hiking the mountain given the conditions. Most thought it would be unwise to go on our own. We agreed and set out to find a guide to help us. We had not used a guide service on past Colorado adventures, so we coupled an internet search with a call to the local REI store, and came up with three potential guides. The first two said they were busy. One of them said he wished he could go because the weather conditions would make it, in his words, "epic." When a mountain guide refers to a hike as "epic," that's probably the moment to reconsider the plan, but there was one more name on the list, so I gave him a call. His name was Dalton and he agreed to take us.

We met Dalton the next morning at 5:00 a.m. His office was on the second floor of a retail building in the small town of Leadville, Colorado. After a quick *hello*, Dalton got right to work explaining the route we would take, checking our gear, asking about our experience as hikers, and explaining his credentials. It was apparent that he knew what he was doing and that we were in good hands. After our initial briefing, we jumped into the truck and drove the handful of snow-covered miles from his office to the trailhead. The parking lot was snow-packed and difficult to navigate, so we found a wide place on the side of the road to safely put the truck, grabbed our packs, and stepped into the cold.

I was a bit apprehensive about the hike, not because of the cold or the snow, but because I'm not good at asking for help. For some reason, the "I don't need a guide" or "we can figure this out on our own" streak runs deep in me. Fortunately, I suppressed my natural inclinations and decided to go with a guide for that day. Dalton proved invaluable in three ways.

1. KNEW THE PATH

From the moment we exited our vehicle, we were breaking trail as the first hikers through the snowy terrain. Much of the route was covered in six inches or more of fresh snow, with some areas holding drifts of at least twenty-four inches. Of course, some areas were relatively barren, but that was because the snow had given way to the forty- to sixty-mile-per-hour winds that plagued most of our hike. Without someone with us who knew the route, we would have had to turn back. I know this because I watched plenty of other hikers turn around that day when they couldn't figure out the best route to the top.

2. TAUGHT US NEW SKILLS

For much of the journey, my head was down to avoid the relentless winds that pelted us with small ice crystals. Clay and I were focused on stepping in the right spots, staying warm, and keeping ourselves moving forward. Although we were experienced hikers, Dalton added to our knowledge by highlighting nuisances of hiking at high altitudes in winter weather. He pointed out how the snow would sweep across the ridgeline and which areas to avoid as the threat of an avalanche grew. He informed us about how to place our feet or best use trekking poles as we moved along. And he showed us how to walk along the ridgeline to avoid the ongoing assault of the prevailing winds as much as possible. These were the winds that caused most hikers to turn back from their summit bid that day.

3. PROVIDED US WITH CONFIDENCE

Dalton also served as a great source of inspiration and confidence. He informed us that we were moving faster than he had anticipated, praised us for getting through some dicey spots, and let us know that we were doing well. Moreover, he led us through the most difficult spots by modeling what he wanted us to do. Seeing him doing it well caused us to see that we could do it, too.

Dalton, Clay, and I were the only people to summit Mt. Sherman that cold and windy day. We could have never done it without him. More importantly, the three of us made it safely back down from the mountain. Getting to the top is only half of the equation.

Many leaders think that they have to go it on their own or feel that asking for guidance is a sign of weakness. Nothing can be further from the truth. Smart leaders understand this. They seek counsel from those with more experience, they observe other leaders in action, and they ask questions to better understand how to handle a given situation. These aren't weak behaviors; they are confidence builders.

DAY 4: FIND GUIDES

Today's Thought

Call the guide whatever you want—coach, mentor, advisor, etc. (yes, I know there are differences)—we all need a guide in our lives.

Today's Questions

1. When you think about your career, whom do you look to for advice and guidance?

   _____

   _____

2. We like to think that we are creating a new path for ourselves and forging new ground, but the reality is that others have gone before us. Who has gone before you that can help you to navigate the path?

   _____

   _____

3. Few things go exactly as planned. You are going to hit the occasional setback, miss an interim goal, or fall short at times. Do you have someone in your life who provides you a needed boost of confidence when times get tough?

   _____

   _____

Today's Challenge

Identify one person who can provide you guidance, direction, or counsel. Send that person a note and set up a time to talk.

DAY 5

SEEK BALANCE

Several years ago, Jamie and I took a business trip to California. On our way to the hotel, we passed a sign proclaiming: "SUP Rental & Instruction, 7 Days a Week."

Not knowing what SUP stood for, we asked our taxi driver. He informed us that it was shorthand for "stand-up paddling." We pulled out our smartphones, did a quick search, and discovered that it was a popular activity up and down the coast.

The activity involves standing upright on a large surfboard-shaped device as you paddle over the water. Done well, it appears nearly effortless with the paddler gliding along the top of the water. Done poorly, it's a struggle with the person spending more time in the water than on top of the board. Either way, it looked fun to us and we asked the driver if he knew of any SUP places close to our hotel.

Fifteen minutes later, we arrived at our hotel armed with the names of several SUP operators in the area and with every intention of SUP-ing during our free time before we left the Golden State. Then, the schedule got away from us. The work side of our trip overwhelmed any personal time. We returned home SUP-less.

Time passed.

Several weeks later, we learned of a SUP location in our hometown of Nashville, Tennessee. No, it wasn't on the ocean like the place in California. Instead, it was on a large lake about twenty minutes from our home, offering a beautiful view in all directions for us to enjoy.

We vowed to make it happen. Then, life got in the way. The summer pace was busier than planned and we spent a great deal of time on the road for work. The summer ended without our SUP adventure.

In a small way, trying to make the SUP adventure happen was a metaphor for the lack of balance in my life. For years, a little one-hour excursion seemed to fall prey to other demands. Granted, if we really wanted to make it happen, we could have forced it into our schedules, but forcing it would have been yet another sign of imbalance.

Over a several-year period, I worked to reduce the forcing function in my life. Frankly, during the first part of my career, I was great at fitting things into my schedule. If there was a white space in the calendar, I filled it in. I spent years physically, mentally, and emotionally sprinting between work and family events. Arriving a few minutes late, my mind often wandered to other pressing issues, instead of fully enjoying the kids' ball games or school plays that were happening right in front of me. I had gotten to the point where I believed that was the way things were supposed to be. I was busy. That was good. The reality was that my beliefs were the problem. I had the wrong mindset when it came to balance. I set out to create a better balance for myself, and the rewards have been manifold.

Consider your own life for a moment.

You have likely had times when you felt out of control; times when the schedule was packed and the pace frantic. The promise you so often heard of work-life balance seemed distant, if not nonexistent.

When I encounter those moments in the future, I will remember SUP. Only this time it stands for:

S - Set Sights
U - Understand Uncomfortableness
P - Purposely Practice

SET SIGHTS

Experience has taught me that much of my out-of-balance feeling stems from having unrealistic expectations or chasing an elusive, perhaps unobtainable, vision of a balanced life. As a leader, you will have to make some sacrifices.

You may not always be home in time for dinner; a last-minute business trip might come about unexpectedly. Depending on the type of work you do, these might be normal occurrences. The key is to be realistic about balance given your situation and communicate it to others in your life to avoid setting unrealistic expectations.

UNDERSTAND UNCOMFORTABLENESS

Doing something new can be a bit uncomfortable. We know this is true when we are acquiring a new skill or taking on a challenging project at work, but the same is true when we are striving for balance in our lives.

Some of us are uncomfortable saying *no* to things, but balance requires doing just that. Trying to please everyone is a sure path to pleasing no one and one of the easiest ways to fall prey to imbalance.

PURPOSELY PRACTICE

The first time you try anything, it can be tough, but when you keep at it, you get better. The mystery of the unexpected is gone and familiarity begins to take hold. With time, your skills will improve. Challenge yourself to purposely set boundaries, to purposely say *no* to tasks that are less important, and to purposely listen to people as opposed to staring at a device.

The reality is that when you seek balance in your life, it takes only a couple of pushes in the right direction to make progress. The first push typically comes when you consider your mindset about creating balance in your life and helping your people to do the same in their lives.

It took a while, but we finally made SUP-ing on the lake happen! We had a great time, and less than a week later, we did it again. The first time out, I considered success having not fallen off the board and making it to the next cove along the lakeshore. Our second outing allowed for quicker speeds and a longer trek across a portion of the lake. It's amazing the balance you can find when you put your mind to it.

DAY 5: SEEK BALANCE

Today's Thought

As a leader, there is more to do every day than you possibly have time to accomplish. Finding balance takes persistence, practice, and courage.

Today's Questions

1. When you work to strike balance, do you set your sights on something realistic and obtainable?

    _____

    _____

2. How uncomfortable are you with disappointing others? How about disappointing yourself?

    _____

    _____

3. What is the last big thing you said *no* to in order to maintain a sense of balance? Did your life blow up or did it continue?

    _____

    _____

4. Are you willing to practice finding balance? Or, will you merely surrender at the first sign of resistance and fall back into old ways?

_____

_____

Today's Challenge

Have a conversation today with a family member or friend about what balance in your work and life should look like from their perspective.

THINK DIFFERENTLY

As a young infantry platoon leader in the United States Army, the majority of my team members were older—some by two decades—and more experienced than me. One day, my platoon was conducting a training exercise where we were patrolling in simulated enemy territory. At one point, the soldier in the front of our patrol (the point person) signaled for everyone to stop. He then gestured that a danger area was in front of us.

Via hand signals, the point person's message silently worked its way through the thirty-nine-person platoon and everyone reacted accordingly. I then made my way to the front of the patrol to assess the situation. As platoon leader, I was expected to determine what we would do next.

Tracking down the lead soldier, I asked why we had stopped. In a low whisper, he explained that there was a large creek to our front. Creeks, roads, open fields, and so on are considered danger areas as they create a place for the enemy to attack. It's desirable to go around or avoid them altogether. If avoiding isn't viable, you try to quickly and safely traverse them. A map check revealed that going around wasn't feasible, so I signaled for a couple of soldiers to position themselves to our left and right flanks. Their job was to watch for enemy activity as their fellow soldiers crossed the creek.

A large log had fallen across the waterway, creating a makeshift bridge. I pointed to the log and suggested that we cross there. I was confident that I had picked the best place.

We began to move.

Within a few meters of the log, the point person again signaled for us to stop. I asked why and he told me that from his now closer perspective, the log didn't look safe. Dismissing his concern, I took the lead myself. Halfway across the log, my sixty-pound pack shifted, I lost my balance, and I fell backward into the creek. I soon found myself fully submerged in nine feet of water.

You are most likely not in the army or foolish enough to charge across a log and fall into a creek. However, you can learn from my mistake. The log incident, coupled with other lessons throughout my career, taught me that leaders must embrace new mindsets. Over the last few days, we have discussed a few of these mindsets. As we get close to ending the first week of the 5 Week Leadership Challenge, I offer five more for your consideration. To help you remember my falling-off-the-log story, and more importantly the five mindsets, I've created an acronym, CREEK.

1. CHECK YOUR EGO

Since you are reading this book and investing in yourself as a leader, I'm confident in saying that you have either received, or are destined to receive, recognition for your leadership potential, track record of results, and growing skill set. Although that type of credit typically leads to getting a formal leadership position, it can also lead to letting your ego get the best of you. You don't have to do it all. You don't have to carry the team on your shoulders. You don't have to set out to prove that you can traverse the log. You don't have to be the hero. Don't let your ego take you there.

2. REMAIN FAIR AND CONSISTENT

This can be tough as leaders can quickly find themselves under pressure to help a friend, bend the rules, or make just one exception. People who were once peers might report to you. Handling the change in the relationship can be tough. Although your intentions might be positive (e.g., wanting to gain support of key team members or trying to make a deposit with a reluctant follower), others might see things in a very different light.

3. EARN RESPECT

Formal authority will only get you so far. People may do what you tell them because you're the leader, but they will likely not give their best. As the expression goes, you can buy someone's back and hands, but you can't buy their head and heart. Heads and hearts are earned when you, as a leader, operate from a position of authentic mutual respect.

It's important to understand and embrace the mindset that respect must be earned through the leader's behavior, not through an organizational coronation. Inhabiting a block in the organizational chart or wearing rank on one's collar does not make you a leader.

Being a leader is a choice and that choice means a willingness to respect others first, to solicit their input, to listen to their ideas, and to create something together. Flexing one's title might garner compliance, but it won't foster commitment. Commitment, much like respect, is earned.

4. ENGAGE PEOPLE

Yes, we touched on this issue in Day 2 this week, but it's worth revisiting again because it so important. One would assume that a new leader who is given a team of smart, capable people would engage them in helping to make decisions. Obvious or not, new leaders—or leaders at any level—often struggle with embracing and engaging others.

Whether it stems from a fear of showing vulnerability, a desire to move quickly and not get bogged down by conversation, or a need to impress, many leaders fail to engage their people in problem solving. Engaging others is one of the best ways for a new leader to learn. Asking questions, listening to understand, and seeking advice all begin with the mindset of engaging others.

Engaging others is not merely about gaining buy-in. It's about creating a better answer. Yes, the leader must make the ultimate decision, but that decision should be informed by the collective wisdom of the team, not the isolated perspective of the leader.

5. KEEP PERSPECTIVE

New leaders can get lost easily in the moment and fail to understand the bigger picture. Perspective matters. Being new in the role, the leader might not realize the cyclical nature of the business or the importance of certain elements. What appears trivial at first blush may prove essential in the long run.

Wisdom often comes with age and experience. Some leaders lack both. However, this doesn't curtail a new leader from being tremendously successful. It simply means that they should embrace a mindset of importance. Doing so is the only way to keep things in perspective.

Spending time understanding what is truly important allows new leaders to put things in perspective. The day-to-day messiness of work might cause them to confuse urgency with importance. Just because a bell rings or a light blinks, they don't have to react. They aren't one of Pavlov's dogs.

After I fell off that fateful log, I somehow managed to suffer no bodily harm and was able to exit the water with all of my equipment. Sopping wet, I crawled up the bank and looked at the point person who had yet to step onto the log. I can still see the well-deserved smirk on his face all these years later. It took a while to dry off, a little longer to regain my pride, and several weeks for the story to dissipate—but it was worth it. I learned a huge lesson about the importance of a leader's mindset.

DAY 6: THINK DIFFERENTLY

Today's Thought

Being a new leader is an exciting, scary, humbling, and amazing time. Embrace it. Keep things in perspective and maintain your balance. And, if you fall off the log, dry yourself off, swallow your pride, and commit to getting it right next time.

Today's Questions

1. When you enter a room, does your ego lead the way or do you leave it in the hall?

    _____

    _____

2. Are there ways you might be failing to be fair and consistent with your people?

    _____

    _____

3. What would you point to in order to show that you are earning, not demanding, respect?

    _____

    _____

4. When was the last time you attempted to truly engage someone else in goal-setting or decisionmaking?

    _____

    _____

5. How well are you keeping things in perspective?

    _____

    _____

Today's Challenge

Based on your answers to the five questions, identify one small but painful action that you can take today to improve in one area.

ENJOY THE JOURNEY

I once found myself in Tanzania setting out to hike to the highest point on the African continent. Don't get me wrong. I didn't suddenly fall from the sky or wake from a dream and find myself on Mt. Kilimanjaro. The prerequisite planning had taken place and I'd put in extra miles to get ready, but on the back end of a busy year and travel delays on our way to Tanzania, I was definitely feeling a bit out of sorts.

Our plane from Chicago to Ethiopia was delayed five hours, causing a cascade of travel problems. Clay and I spent twenty-four hours on the ground in Ethiopia's capital city, Addis Ababa, and arrived a day late to Tanzania. Normally this wouldn't be a big deal, but our tardiness meant that the entire hike might have been in jeopardy. When we arrived at Kilimanjaro International Airport, we headed straight to baggage claim. There we found a man with a slight build and broad smile waiting for us. His name was Rashid and he would be our guide. After exchanging pleasantries, he asked what we wanted to do since our schedule was messed up.

"Let's go climb the mountain," I said. He seemed a bit surprised that Clay and I wanted to go straight to the mountain because it was late in the day and we had miles to hike—miles that we would have tackled early that morning had we arrived on time the previous day.

We grabbed our stuff, jumped into the truck, and headed to the entrance gate. Rashid was on the phone for much of the ride speaking in Swahili, while our driver, John, headed straight to the mountain. We later learned that Rashid was negotiating with the authorities to keep the gate open until we arrived. Apparently, he was able to convince them. As soon as John wheeled our truck through the gate at the base of the mountain, it was locked behind us. We grabbed our gear, changed our clothes, did a quick inventory of our supplies, and headed out just as the rain started and night fell. We briskly hiked through the forest for the next several hours, dodging puddles, slipping occasionally, and gradually growing accustomed to the monkeys shrieking in the darkness.

When we arrived at camp, Rashid introduced us to his assistant, Harold. Both were Kilimanjaro pros, having summited the 19,341-foot (5,895-meter) peak nearly three hundred times each. Over the course of the next five days, their job was to provide the help and direction that Clay and I needed in order to achieve our goal of summiting the mountain and safely returning to the bottom.

I love setting goals, accomplishing them, and then checking them off of my list. It feeds me. Frankly, that's one of the things that attracts me to hiking. I think to myself, "There's the mountain. Here's how tall it is. Let's tackle this thing and knock it off our list."

Each night, our guides, Rashid and Harold, would brief us on the next day's hike. It usually took place right after we finished dinner. They would enter the tent and talk to us about the plan for the next day, addressing the terrain, anticipated weather, elevation changes, and where we would camp that next night.

I would inevitably ask questions about the top of the mountain. I would inquire how many miles would be left to the top of the mountain after the next day's hike, or whether the plans meant we only had a certain distance left to go.

In his unflappable manner, Rashid would remind me that we take it one day at a time on the mountain. His point was that I shouldn't fixate on getting to the top, because doing so could jeopardize everything. He wanted us to focus on the journey, to enjoy it, and to cherish the memories we were making. Rashid would remind me to enjoy the vegetation and take in the changing terrain as we hiked through the five distinct zones of the mountain, ranging from countryside slopes to the arctic ice cap found at the summit.

Rashid was right. I knew he was right, but there was always a small part of me that longed to check the mountain off of my to-do list. In his wisdom, he kept grounding me in the moment. He knew from years on the mountain that focusing on the long-term goal caused many hikers to fail in the short term.

The same can be true for leaders. When you are in a leadership role, you might find yourself constantly focusing on the next goal on the list, the next project to deliver, or the next set of numbers to meet. This can happen for a number of reasons. You may be like me and enjoy checking items off of your to-do list. Perhaps you find yourself in a high-pressure work environment that is causing an overemphasis on delivering results and an underemphasis on developing people. Maybe you are underresourced and yearning for a future state. Whatever the reason, it's important to do what you can to maintain perspective and remember that you, too, are on a journey. Take time to pause, live in the moment, and enjoy the ride.

Eventually, Clay and I made it to the top of Mt. Kilimanjaro safely and returned without incident to the base of the mountain. Along the way, I let go of asking some (not all) of the questions about the distance to the top of the mountain. I allowed myself to enjoy the moment in the moment. We had an amazing time.

After our return to the United States, I found myself focusing not on the 19,341-foot summit, but on the pictures and videos we captured along the way. It's those memories, not checking the mountain off of my to-do list, that made everything worthwhile.

DAY 7: ENJOY THE JOURNEY

Today's Thought

If you fast-forward ten, fifteen, twenty, or more years, you and those on your team won't remember the specific goals you are working on today. No one will recall the metrics that are driving today's discussions, but they will remember what it was like to work with you. They will remember what it was like having you as a leader.

Today's Questions

1. How might your focus on tasks, goals, objectives, and results be causing you to lose sight of the bigger perspective?

   _____

   _____

2. How often do you take the time to pause in the moment and enjoy the journey?

   _____

   _____

3. What might you do differently to enjoy the moment, while delivering results?

   _____

   _____

Today's Challenge

Make a commitment to pause three times today and reflect on the moment. On the next page, you'll find the Week 1 Wrap-up; before you begin, jot down what you observed, heard, felt, and so on. Then, think what you would have missed if you hadn't spent that moment in the moment.

WEEK 1 WRAP-UP

T hroughout the course of this week, you explored ten leadership mindsets. Now is a chance for you to assess your current thinking in each area. Consider if you are on target, struggling, or somewhere in between.

TEN LEADERSHIP MINDSETS

Clarify Focus (Day 1)

Engage People (Day 2)

Rethink Failure (Day 3)

Find Guides (Day 4)

Seek Balance (Day 5)

Check Ego (Day 6)

Remain Consistent (Day 6)

Earn Respect (Day 6)

Keep Things in Context (Day 6)

Enjoy the Journey (Day 7)

Mindset		Your Current Thinking											
Clarify Focus	Struggling	0	1	2	3	4	5	6	7	8	9	10	On Target
Engage People	Struggling	0	1	2	3	4	5	6	7	8	9	10	On Target
Rethink Failure	Struggling	0	1	2	3	4	5	6	7	8	9	10	On Target
Find Guides	Struggling	0	1	2	3	4	5	6	7	8	9	10	On Target
Seek Balance	Struggling	0	1	2	3	4	5	6	7	8	9	10	On Target
Check Ego	Struggling	0	1	2	3	4	5	6	7	8	9	10	On Target
Remain Consistent	Struggling	0	1	2	3	4	5	6	7	8	9	10	On Target
Earn Respect	Struggling	0	1	2	3	4	5	6	7	8	9	10	On Target
Keep Things in Context	Struggling	0	1	2	3	4	5	6	7	8	9	10	On Target
Enjoy the Journey	Struggling	0	1	2	3	4	5	6	7	8	9	10	On Target

Considering how you assessed yourself, answer the following questions:

Do you believe that others would agree with your assessment? Why or why not?

_____

_____

_____

_____

_____

For the areas that you assess as currently on target, what can you do to sustain them?

_____

_____

_____

_____

_____

For those mindsets where you are struggling, which one would you like to address first? What can you do to begin to shift your thinking?

_____

_____

_____

_____

DISCOVER PURPOSE

The sign above the entrance read "Disco Hut," but I was convinced it wasn't a place for dancing, partying, or any form of enjoyment. The approximately 400-square-foot (37.2-square-meter) building was made of cinderblock and had no windows. It wasn't cute, quaint, or inviting and neither was its inhabitant. The hut's door swung open and a figure emerged from the fog bellowing out of the structure. He was wearing a mask and hood, gloves, boots, and a protective suit. He positioned himself in front of the group and removed his mask in a dramatic gesture designed to capture our absolute attention. He introduced himself as our instructor for the day and began to explain what we were about to do. I recognized the instructor as a drill sergeant from another platoon. Past encounters with him had not been pleasant.

Allow me to give a bit of background. The year was 1987. I was eighteen years old and about midway through United States Army basic training at

Ft. McClellan, Alabama. The month was June and the temperature was off the charts hot, but our instructor didn't seem to mind the heat even in the heavy suit he was wearing. The smirk on his face as he addressed us, coupled with the words coming out of his mouth, revealed the source of his pleasant disposition. He was about to make our lives miserable.

He told us that we were to put on our gas masks and enter the Disco Hut in groups of five. Explaining that the room was filled with CS gas (tear gas), the instructor told us that we would feel a burning sensation on our exposed skin, but the "real fun" as he called it, would happen when each of us would be required to remove our mask and tell him our name, rank, and identification number. He said that's when you will realize why this building is called the Disco Hut. At this point, the smirk gave way to a full-on smile. You might want to see a friend or family member smile, but experience had taught me that causing a U.S. Army drill sergeant to smile was not something you cherished. Those smiles always came at a cost.

Before we launched into the activity, our host asked, "Does anyone have any questions?" They always asked us this question before we set out on our next task, but it was intended to be rhetorical. Trust me, they had no interest in responding to our inquiries. We knew this and went along with the charade of a drill sergeant asking if we had questions by providing the expected silence in response.

Of course we had questions; we just didn't ask them—at least we typically didn't ask anything. In this instance, one brave soul must have raised his hand. I didn't see it because I was fixated on the instructor and processing what was about to happen, but someone in the formation raised his hand. No doubt he caught the drill sergeant off guard as it was a blatant violation of the unspoken process.

The drill sergeant barked, "I see someone has a question. Yes, Private, what do you want?" A voice in the crowd responded with a hesitant, "Why are we doing this, Drill Sergeant?"

Our instructor must have been impressed by the question. Not only did he provide an immediate response of, "Because I'm telling you to do it," but he also rewarded the inquisitive private by letting him jump to the front of the line and be the first that day to enter the Disco Hut.

The private who asked the drill sergeant the question some thirty years ago might have been a bit naive in asking given the conditions at the time, but his question was one that all of us wanted answered. We wanted to understand why. Under different circumstances, we would have likely received a more nuanced and informed response recognizing the discomfort of the pending tear gas with a reminder that the mask would prove to be an effective barrier. It was a training exercise to ingrain in us the importance of the protective gear.

No doubt this answer to the *why* question would have been far more helpful to all of us.

My point is that people want to know the *why* behind the actions we ask them to take, the priorities we set for and with them, and the outcomes we strive to accomplish. It has to run deeper than "because I told you to do it." The same is true for you as a leader. It's important for you to explore why you lead. Understanding your leadership motivation will go a long way when times are tough, when you are tired, and when big obstacles stand between you and your goals. This week is all about exploring your why and defining your leadership purpose.

Just in case you are wondering, I figured out why they called it the "Disco Hut." Upon entering the poorly lit chamber, I took my place in the middle of a row of five soldiers. One by one, the drill sergeant stood in front of each of us and with a muffled voice told us to remove our mask and provide him the information he requested. My peripheral vision was good enough to watch the movements to my left as the first two soldiers removed their masks and recited the required information. It wasn't pretty. After their initial oxygen supply was depleted and they gasped for more air, the CS hit them and they were looking for the door. That's what happened to me, too. I said my name, rank, and a portion of some number and gave the drill sergeant every indication that I was ready to hit the Disco Hut dance floor. My legs were moving, my eyes were watering, and my hands were shaking. He pointed to the exit, barked, "Get out of here, Private," and I stumbled toward the light. Once outside, I was instructed to flap my arms like a bird, not to touch my face, and to walk in circles around a tree until I felt better. Then, I could rinse my eyes and get back into formation.

In 1999, Ft. McClellan, Alabama, was officially closed after eighty-one years of training soldiers. I can't help but imagine that, as the post closed, someone managed to snag the Disco Hut sign. I hope that it's hanging in someone's house as a tribute to those who experienced the tear gas–fueled dance party that I had encountered. When others see the sign and learn about its history, I can't help but hear their question: "And *why* did they do that?"

Keeping a clear purpose in front of you and your team is paramount to moving forward together and accomplishing the goals you set forth. You cannot expect those you lead to blindly follow tasks without a reason to propel them from one step to the next. Discovering your purpose as a leader is an essential endeavor to put into practice leading others to understand their own purpose and role.

EXCAVATE PURPOSE

n 1981, Indiana Jones ran, swung, and fought his way into movie theaters. Since then, the archeologist has taken audiences on numerous epic adventures in search of hidden treasure. You are likely familiar with the basic Indiana Jones story line. After painstaking effort, dangerous encounters ("Snakes . . . why'd it have to be snakes?"), and finding himself at the precipice of failure, Jones evades all that is stacked against him and unearths the buried treasure. Jones is an extraordinary archeologist who has captured the fascination of audiences everywhere.

I am fortunate to know an archeologist who also captures the attention of audiences. Millions of theatergoers don't buy tickets to his movies and his work doesn't involve navigating his way through dangerous catacombs, but he is an archeologist nonetheless. Well, at least an archeologist of a sort. His name is Brad White and he is the president of Europe + Middle East at Brighthouse, a Boston Consulting Group (BCG) Company. Most semesters, Brad visits my classroom at Vanderbilt University and shares how he and his Brighthouse colleagues go on archeological explorations with organizations to excavate for purpose.

Humans need oxygen, water, food, and sleep. According to Brad, we have a similar need for purpose. We need to make sense of things, to understand the deeper meaning, and to uncover the purpose of something.

As a natural extension of the idea that individuals search for meaning, a team or organization (which is composed of people) yearns for a clear purpose, too. Having one is what allows a team or organization to better understand the culture it is building, the products it creates, the services it renders, and the customers it serves.

Brad explains that nearly every organization, large or small, started with an implicit purpose. Someone saw a need in the world, determined that they had the ability to fill the need, and put resources to work to solve the problem. As is often the case, time passes, changes ensue, employees come and go, and people lose the connection to the organization's core purpose.

Brad says that when this happens, an archeologist is needed to help an organization rediscover its purpose and then to share the purpose with others so that employees and customers can reconnect with it. Having a clear purpose can help an organization to win on key metrics like return to shareholders, revenue growth, employee engagement, and customer retention.

The same can be argued for leaders, as they must also find greater meaning in their work. Career advancement, a bigger paycheck, and more influence in the organization can all be alluring, but those are not the ultimate sources of meaning. Leadership is tough. At times it is exhausting, frustrating, and downright unenjoyable. And it's during those challenging times that you need to be able to draw energy from a deep reservoir of purpose. Call it a purpose decree, a leadership impact statement, or a meaning mantra, but you need to make one and there is no better time than now to do it. So, take yourself on an epic adventure to uncover why you choose to lead.

Beware, there's some bad news with purpose (there always has to be snakes). The bad news comes in two forms. First, as you excavate your purpose and work to live it out in your work and life, it will require you to say *no* to some things. These are things that aren't aligned to your purpose or have the potential to pull you in the wrong direction. This would be easy to accomplish if all of these things were bad things, because we can understand that saying *no* to bad thing is a good thing to do. However, many of the things that you have to say *no* to are good things. Consider an athlete who determines that her purpose includes representing her country in the Olympic games. In order to achieve this, she will have to say *no* to many good things ranging from hanging out with friends so she can get a solid night's sleep or closely managing her diet and saying *no* to an extra slice of cake. As good as some of those things may be in the moment, they aren't aligned to her long-term vision for herself.

Second, staying true to your purpose is fraught with missteps, no matter how motivating the meaning or strong your will is. You are human. You will mess up. You will let the day-to-day cause you to lose sight of your purpose at times. In turn, you will make choices that you later regret. The key isn't to always make the exact right choice. Hold yourself to that standard and you are going to be disappointed. The key is do your best in every moment to operate in alignment with your purpose, and when you mess up to ensure that you do the next right thing.

This week you will work on your purpose, but never forget that excavating purpose isn't a one-day or one-week activity. It takes prolonged and serious effort. You will make tremendous progress this week if you stick to the challenge, but know that once the challenge is over, you must continue to revisit, refine, and reflect on your purpose.

DAY 8: EXCAVATE PURPOSE

Today's Thought

Understanding purpose facilitates your ability to make the right decisions, take the right actions, and model the right behaviors, especially in tough times.

Today's Questions

Think about a team that you have been on in the past that had a very clear purpose. This could be a team from work, school, sports, or what have you.

1. How did having a clear purpose affect the energy level of the team?

_____

_____

2. How committed were you and your teammates to the team's success?

_____

_____

3. What was the team able to achieve as a result of the clear purpose?

_____

_____

Today's Challenge

Meet with two people and ask each to share a time when they were on a team that had a clear purpose. As they share their stories, listen for examples of energy, commitment, and results. Doing this will allow you to see firsthand the power of purpose.

**DAY
9**

UNDERSTAND MEANING

W hen my daughter, Alex, asked me if I would run a half marathon with her, I agreed without hesitation. I knew that I would relish the opportunity to train and run the 13.1-mile (21-kilometer) race with her. The weekend that we chose for the race offered events in several cities within driving distance of our homes, each designed to support a different charitable cause. As we looked at our options, we selected an inaugural 5K/half marathon to be held in Memphis, Tennessee. The race was part of the Civil Rights Race Series and was intended to support economic development for underserved communities, educate people on several historical events, and promote health and wellness in the surrounding communities.

We felt good about our decision to run the race together and the cause we were supporting. We were motivated. When the race weekend arrived, we made the three-hour drive from Nashville to Memphis, ate a pasta dinner, and got to bed early. The next morning, we left our hotel and made the short half-mile (0.8-kilometer) walk to the starting line.

As we approached the site, we saw about eighty people milling about in the parking lot adjacent to the National Civil Rights Museum. The museum is located at the former Lorraine Motel, the location where Dr. Martin Luther King Jr. was assassinated in 1968. The city was inspiring, and those preparing to run the race were motivated. The size of the crowd seemed small, especially since it was both a 5K and a half marathon, but it was the inaugural race and we didn't think much about it.

As the race's start time approached, we noticed a group of women posing for a picture with their medals. We also noticed that we didn't see a start or finish line. Nor did we hear an announcer or any upbeat music. We definitely noticed that things were different from past races we completed. Normally, you receive medals after the race and the music is typically cranked up to get the runners excited.

The race start time came and went and nothing changed. People were still wandering around and chatting. Eventually, a line formed in front of a makeshift table where volunteers were handing out medals to all of the runners. We joined the line of those making their way to the medals table. I turned to another runner and inquired about the situation. He informed me that the race had been canceled. Apparently, something was wrong with the route permit and the city told the race organizers that they couldn't host the event.

After we picked up our medals, I turned to Alex and said, "Well, we signed up for this thing, trained for it, and drove all the way over. We might as well do it." She agreed. We walked back to our hotel and dropped our medals off at the front desk. We knew better than to go back to our rooms where our beds awaited us. Then we headed off on our own 13.1-mile trek through the streets of Memphis with our race numbers still affixed to our T-shirts.

Over the course of the next couple of hours, we encountered several runners doing their own races. They were also proudly displaying their Civil Rights Race Series race bibs on their shirts. Occasionally, we would strike up a conversation with a fellow runner. Along the way, we met people from Georgia, Ohio, and as far away as California. All had traveled to Memphis to run the race and show their support for the cause. Surprisingly, no one complained about the race being canceled. Everyone seemed genuinely happy to be there. They were making the most of the cancellation.

I marveled at how someone could invest their time and money to travel hundreds of miles to run a race on a hot Saturday morning, and not be angry that the run was canceled.

As I ran and thought about it more, I realized three things:

1. They weren't doing it for comfort, as there were no water stations or food tables offering much-needed nourishment.
2. They weren't doing it for a pat on the back, as there were no supporters on the route to cheer us on.

3. They weren't doing it for the race medal, as we already had that before we started.

When I asked people about their positive attitude given the situation, *all* of the runners conveyed a similar sentiment. We were all disappointed the race was canceled and the running conditions weren't ideal, but it was for a good cause.

Is it possible that their motivation stemmed from the deep meaning they found in the event's purpose?

I think so.

They had invested the time to prepare. They had committed themselves to running the race. They felt the run's cause was worthy and important.

There is a tremendous amount of energy, passion, and enthusiasm that comes when people find meaning.

The same is true in your work. When you find meaning in your work and help others to do the same, people will run through walls—or the streets of Memphis—to make things happen. Don't miss the chance to tap into that power.

DAY 9: UNDERSTAND MEANING

Today's Thought

Finding meaning in your work is what allows you and your team to overcome the day-to-day challenges of work. It's not the other way around.

Today's Questions

1. How would you describe the meaning that you find in your work?

   _____

   _____

2. When was the last time you tapped into motivation that flows from an important cause? How would you describe the feeling?

   _____

   _____

3. How well do the people you work with understand the purpose behind what they do?

   _____

   _____

Today's Challenge

As you go through the workday, pause occasionally and reflect on your energy level. Make note of times when you feel most energized and ask yourself what it is about what you are doing in the moment that is causing your energy to spike.

DAY
10

UNCOVER PROBLEMS

E very semester, my undergraduate marketing students work with a business, nonprofit, or university organization to gain hands-on experience in a real-world environment. In past semesters, students have supported a training company's efforts to better understand customer needs, improved a university athletic program's fan appreciation package, assisted an entrepreneur in launching a new consumer product, and partnered with a scholarship program to increase their number of applications. These experiences allow students the chance to explore customer needs, research solutions, and present recommended courses of action to their clients.

At the beginning of the semester, students assess themselves in the areas of creativity, research, analysis, and communication. Those assessments are used to form complementary teams in which the strengths of one member makes the weaknesses of another immaterial. Although building great student teams and stewarding their efforts throughout the course of the semester is important, it's insufficient if I'm unable to find great clients for them to support. The journey to find such a client begins well before the start of the semester and involves a screening process where I meet with potential clients to understand their business needs and to convey my expectations for the semester. As you might imagine, these projects require a client who is open to working with students, clear on their priorities, realistic about what is achievable, and consistently accessible to student groups. The client must also be willing to come to campus at the beginning of the semester to tell their story to the students and return at the end to receive the final presentations. When a good client is matched with a strong team, the results are amazing.

Jen Auerbach and Adriel Denae have proven themselves to be a dream client. They show students the importance of uncovering and addressing problems. Jen and Adriel own Clary Collection, a skin- and body-care company in Nashville, Tennessee. In 2016, the cofounders and friends were both expecting their first children and struggling to find the best way to care for themselves throughout their pregnancies. They quickly discovered that providing the level of self-care they desired was more difficult than expected as product labels were often misleading, brand promises underperformed, and items that did work were simply unavailable. Jen and Adriel set out to solve the problem themselves. They studied recipes, tested production methods, and concocted creations in Jen's kitchen. They used their homemade skin-care products on themselves and shared them with friends who were facing similar problems. The response was overwhelming and they expanded production to meet the growing demand. Eventually Jen and Adriel moved from the kitchen to an old barn, sourced raw materials in bulk, designed packaging, built a website, and began to sell their products online to a growing list of raving fans.

Their efforts to tackle and solve a problem that they were passionate about took them from testing products in their kitchens to being featured in *Vanity Fair*, *Vogue*, *InStyle*, and numerous other publications. They have created a line of balms, bath-and-body oil, and other skin-care products. These items, made for moms by moms, are beautifully packaged in 1930s-style containers demonstrating that their products are both timeless and timely. Along the way, the duo has created tote bags and T-shirts featuring the expression "Naturally Empowering Women." The items are intended to motivate, inspire, and support female entrepreneurs who are striving to get their own businesses off the ground and to solve problems that they see in the lives of their customers. Jen and Adriel have also shared a portion of the proceeds with a women's shelter to help others who are facing personal challenges.

As my students work with Jen and Adriel, the importance of awareness and action become apparent. I explain that we often fail on both fronts by missing problems that are right in front of us and failing to address a problem when it is uncovered. This reality is true from business decisions to minute daily tasks in our personal lives. To drive the point home, I tell my students a story about building a house.

In the first several years of our marriage, Jamie and I created a wish list of all the things we wanted in a future house. When the time came to build it, she and I went into painstaking detail with the architect about the number of bedrooms, size of the kitchen, color of the brick, and on and on. When construction started, we watched the builder as he and his team prepared the land, framed the building, and completed every construction step. We drove by the construction site several times a week to check on the progress and to ensure that all was on track. Occasionally, we found a problem—the wrong tile around the fireplace or a light fixture in the wrong location. When these situations occurred, we would contact the builder and he quickly fixed it. The process went well. When the house was finished, we completed the closing paperwork and started moving boxes. The first day was exciting and exhausting. We unpacked box after box, ate pizza at a makeshift cardboard table, and collapsed on our mattress well after midnight, too tired to assemble the bed frame. The next morning, I woke up early in an effort to pick up where we left off. I started by gathering the packing materials that were scattered about and taking them to the yard via the garage. As I reached for the button to open the garage door, I realized that it was mounted well beyond my reach. It wasn't even close. So, I grabbed a broom handle and used it to reach the button. The makeshift solution wasn't pretty, but it worked. The door went up. I then thought about all the times we had gone out to the job site with the intent of finding problems along the way, and we missed an obvious deficiency. I explain to the students that this is an example of my failing to uncover a problem. I had walked in and out of that garage twenty times and never looked at the door opener.

Then I tell them the rest of the story. We lived in that home for three years before we fixed the problem. The four of us went in and out of that garage countless times and we never moved the garage door opener. True, the makeshift broom handle solution had morphed over the years to a more eloquent device better suited for the job—a long-handled ice scraper—but we never moved the opener. It wasn't until a friend was visiting. He discovered the problem, and with his prodding, we fixed it. The solution took us about twenty minutes.

As you work to discover your underlying purpose as a leader, it's important to stop and think through questions about the problems around you, and your willingness to address them.

DAY 10: UNCOVER PROBLEMS

Today's Thought

Uncovering and working to solve a problem can often ignite one's passion and fuel one's purpose.

Today's Questions

1. What problems do you see around you that need addressing?

    _____

    _____

2. Of those problems, which one are you uniquely positioned to solve?

    _____

    _____

3. Is there one of these problems you're passionate about solving?

    _____

    _____

Today's Challenge

Spend five minutes brainstorming what would happen if one of the problems you listed above was solved. Make note of what opportunities would arise and what pains or struggles would be relieved.

DAY 11

ASSESS TALENT

During the eleven-year period that we owned our business, we would hold an annual meeting every winter. It was the one time of the year when all of our employees met in the same location. It offered us the invaluable opportunity to connect, plan, celebrate, and learn. I always looked forward to those meetings, knowing that we gained so much from getting the entire team together.

One year we went to Orlando, Florida, and stayed at the Walt Disney World Resort, splitting our time between meetings during the day and activities in the evening. I'll never forget the night when we descended upon the Magic Kingdom and conducted a scavenger hunt in teams of three. The look of joy on my colleagues' faces when they discovered an object on their scavenger list was only overshadowed by the reactions of the other park guests who were clearly confused by three grown adults high-fiving after grabbing a spork from a quick service restaurant. Another year we went to Washington, D.C., where we held our meetings for two days, enjoyed a number of great meals, and took in the sights of the nation's capital.

I truly mean it when I say that I treasured our annual meetings because each session produced a wonderful mix of business outcomes and team memories. However, there is one session that was most memorable to me, and arguably changed the trajectory of the company. It occurred when we held an annual conference in Louisville, Kentucky. We toured Churchill Downs, the home of the Kentucky Derby, and saw the fabled track and the museum. But the pivotal moment for our company occurred not on the iconic racetrack, but in a historic hotel a couple of miles up the road. Since the mid-1800s, the Seelbach Hotel has sat on Fourth Street near the heart of town. The hotel has a storied past as a refuge for bootleggers and mobsters throughout the Prohibition era and is the rumored inspiration behind F. Scott Fitzgerald's *The Great Gatsby*. In fact, a documentary was once made about the hidden tunnels that supposedly could facilitate Al Capone's escape out of the ornate dining room if the authorities showed up on the premises. The Seelbach is equal parts folklore and festive.

I wish I could tell you that the big moment for our firm occurred in a catacomb deep in the bowels of the 150-year-old lodge where, while conducting a scavenger hunt, I discovered a treasure hidden behind a loose brick. The reality is that I was wearing a sports coat and presenting PowerPoint slides in a conference room on the second floor, not spelunking in the basement. But we did discover an amazing treasure of sorts hidden right below the surface.

We had assembled at 8:00 a.m. that morning to tackle the day's agenda. About two hours into the discussion and just before a much-needed break, I was wrapping up my comments about what we had accomplished that year. The year in review presentation had gone well because I had great material to work with. The business was growing, our customers were proving very loyal to us, and we had added some great new members to our team. As a leader, it was a slam-dunk, let's-celebrate kind of year. That is until one of my colleagues asked a great question. While most of us were looking to wrap up the presentation and head to the restroom, the snack cart, or both, a person from our Washington, D.C., office asked, "We definitely had a great year and we are growing, but what is it that we are truly exceptional at?"

That simple question changed everything.

The break was postponed without objection and the day's agenda was tossed out without a word as my teammate's inquiry launched the room into a rich, important, and long-overdue conversation. One by one, team members provided their take on the question. In general, people fell into one of two camps. Those in one camp pointed to the work we had historically accomplished and said that we are best defined by the work that we do. Those in the other camp focused on the industry we operated in, explaining that our business had grown as a result of referrals from one client to another, all of which operated in the same industry. Therefore, we were defined not by what we do but by whom we do it for. We had paid the price to understand the needs of our clients and our value came from those insights.

The conversation continued well through lunch with everyone stating (and at times restating) their answers, but no response seemed to satisfy the question that began the debate. Clearly, the consensus was that having work to do and having customers to pay for the work were both important, but neither seemed to provide a great connection to the unique abilities of those sitting in the room that day. It was obvious that satisfactorily answering the question my colleague posed would require us to dig deep into our unique talents, allowing us to determine what it was that we best provided to the world. So, we turned the question around on ourselves by asking what our individual and collective strengths, skills, and capabilities were. Moreover, how could we bring those talents to the forefront of our work? Our answers to those questions allowed us to see what was possible and where gaps in our current team existed.

Up until the point when we had this conversation, we were doing good work and making our financial numbers, but we weren't necessarily tapping into our full talent as a team or delivering the best work we could for the world.

The same is true for you. You may be busy doing work and you may be drawing a decent paycheck, but neither is necessarily indicative of your unique talents. As we work this week to discover your purpose as a leader, we have to dig deeper than job descriptions, task lists, and pay stubs. In doing so, you have to explore talents that may be lying beneath the surface.

For Wedgewood Consulting Group, being clear on what we were truly good at and the value we provided changed everything. It allowed us to determine what gaps we had in our knowledge, skills, and abilities. It allowed us to hire new people who would add new strengths to the team and who made our weaknesses irrelevant. It allowed us to better focus our efforts by knowing what work we would pursue and what we would let go.

DAY 11: ASSESS TALENT

Today's Thought

You possess unique talents, skills, and capabilities. One of your jobs as a leader is to build a team around you that complements those strengths and collectively makes individual weaknesses irrelevant.

Today's Questions

1. What have others told you are your professional and personal strengths?

    _____

    _____

2. What work task or activity are you most confident performing?

    _____

    _____

3. What are the two or three talents that you believe you uniquely possess?

    _____

    _____

Today's Challenge

Talk to two or three colleagues, friends, or family members and ask each one this question: "What are the two or three talents that you believe I uniquely possess?"

Take note of their responses and compare them to your answers to today's questions.

EXPLORE PASSION

A manufacturing company in Southern California once hired me to teach a leadership workshop for a group of production supervisors and project managers. Over the course of three days, I worked with twenty-four new and aspiring leaders in an effort to help them to be more effective in their roles. I truly enjoy facilitating these sessions as I have the chance to work closely with people who are excited to learn, are dealing with real problems—and, most importantly, want to take action. As much as I enjoy these sessions, today's lesson is not about what happened in the leadership workshop. It's about what transpired each day before I arrived at the client site. It's about a leadership lesson I learned that week.

Southern California is known for its legendary traffic jams and slow commutes. My hotel was located eight miles (thirteen kilometers) from the client site and I wasn't sure how long it would take, so at the guidance of my client I gave myself plenty of time to get there. As fate would have it, traffic was light and I arrived in less than fifteen minutes, turning into the company's parking lot a full two hours before the start of my presentation. Having not had my morning coffee yet, I pulled out my phone, opened my Starbucks app, and found the closest location. Luckily, it was right around the corner. I made the short commute, grabbed my morning beverage, and arrived back at the client site with plenty of time to spare.

On day two, I left my hotel a bit later but ensured that I had time to get to Starbucks. Everything worked as planned and I arrived at the client site thirty minutes early, drink in hand. On the third day, I set out to repeat my day two performance, but I hit a snag when the Starbucks was closed because of a broken pipe. A makeshift sign taped to the front window made the solemn announcement. I'm no quitter, so I pulled out my trusty Starbucks app only to find that the nearest store was several miles away. Doing a bit of mental math, I realized that I couldn't make the round trip on time. So, I jumped into my rental car and set out with the hopes of finding a reasonable alternative in the general area.

I turned out of the Starbucks parking lot onto a major thoroughfare and stayed in the right lane with my eyes peeled for a coffee shop. Time was ticking and I was about to give up when I spotted a small storefront in the middle of a strip mall. I turned into the lot, found a parking spot, and briskly walked to the front door.

The aroma of fresh-brewed coffee hit me as I stepped into the one-of-a-kind establishment. Five minutes later, I emerged from the business with my coffee in hand. Everything went better than I expected: the place was clean and the coffee proved to be good, but what stuck with me was my conversation with the woman behind the counter.

Upon entering the shop and walking up to the register, I was met with a pleasant smile and a kind, "Good morning, how may I help you today?" from the barista. The name tag on her smock read "Helpful Helen" in lettering so neat that I looked twice to confirm it was actually handwritten. As I watched Helen perform her duties, it became apparent to me that she was living up to her name.

- I was unfamiliar with the menu—Helen was helpful and patient.
- Numerous people were crowding the café, many sending off signals of being in a rush—yet Helen was helpful and efficient.
- A customer asked for directions to a nearby business—Helen was helpful and informative.

Although I appreciated her service, what struck me was her passion. The place was busy that day; I imagine it is busy most every day. However, as customer after customer came to the counter, Helen greeted each with a smile, called many by name, connected with everyone in the moment, and seemed to make each person feel special. She knew her customers and they seemed to appreciate the way she treated each one of them.

When I thanked her for her service, she looked at me and said, "You're very welcome. It was a pleasure to serve you today and I hope to see you in the future."

I responded, "Well, the next time I'm in town, I will certainly come here for my coffee and perhaps one of your breakfast sandwiches," pointing to the food her coworker was preparing to Helen's left. I quickly added, "You truly seem to enjoy your job."

In all sincerity, Helpful Helen replied, "There are lots of things I can do in life, but I've realized that my biggest contribution comes from serving the people who come through our door every morning and making their day a bit brighter. I am passionate about doing that!"

Helpful Helen had me. The next time I come to town, I will make it a point to visit this little shop. She wasn't merely serving coffee; she was choosing to make a positive impact on every person who walked through the door.

Helen had a rare gift. She knew what she was passionate about, found a place where she could make a big contribution, and was actively working to make a difference in the lives of her customers. She recognized that while some customers were in a rush as they started their day, others were looking for a bit of conversation. Some were unfamiliar with the shop and needed a bit more guidance, and others were regulars who didn't need to utter a word as Helen knew what they needed. Her ability to meet everyone's expectations and the desire to do it with excellence stemmed from the meaning she found in her work.

Perhaps you are thinking to yourself, "I'm glad Patrick had a pleasant experience, but I don't run a small coffee shop. Our work and people are far removed from Helen's world."

Regardless of what you do and whom you work with, I think we would all agree that having more competent, confident, committed, and contributing people in our organizations would be a wonderful thing.

What would it mean to you and your organization if you had a culture of Helens? You would end up with a culture of passionate contributors striving to bring their best to every meeting, every customer touch point, every task, every day.

DAY 12: EXPLORE PASSION

Today's Thought

Every person you meet is passionate about something. The ones who are the most fulfilled are those who have found a role that allows them to get paid to pursue their passions.

Today's Questions

1. What energizes you?

_____

_____

2. What drains your energy?

_____

_____

3. What type of work would you do regardless of the pay?

_____

_____

Today's Challenge

Set a timer for two minutes and write freely about your passions. There is no right or wrong answer. Just let your thoughts flow onto the paper.

**DAY
13**

CLOSE DOORS

Years ago, I was working on my doctorate at the University of Kentucky. Classes were held in person at the school's main campus, which was exactly 63 miles (101.4 kilometers) from my house. For three years of in-person classes and two years of dissertation work, I drove the 126-mile (203-kilometer) round trip some 250 times. The Kentucky countryside was beautiful and I enjoyed the horse farms as I made the commute, but it had gotten to the point that I could easily describe every bump, turn, and scenic view along the winding path from the front door of my house to the classroom.

Although many doctoral students attend school as their full-time endeavor, I opted to continue running our company as I completed my studies. We had a lot of interesting work going on in our business at the time, the company was growing, and employees in our offices in Dayton, OH; Washington, D.C.; and Louisville, KY counted on my daily involvement. On a typical week, I would put in more than forty hours for work and another twenty or more on school. It wasn't uncommon for me to work in Louisville on Monday until 3:00 p.m., drive to campus for a class that evening, catch a flight to D.C. after class, work in D.C. until noon on Wednesday, catch a flight back to campus for a Wednesday night class, and drive up to Ohio on Thursday for a quick overnight trip. Weekends and free evenings were packed with homework.

By any measure, I had way too much on my plate with school and work. Add to the mix that Jamie and I were doing our best to raise our children (who were then eight and thirteen years old) and keep our marriage on track. Nonetheless, I kept saying *yes* to side projects and I became involved in a nonprofit. I was very busy.

I share all of this not out of pride, but embarrassment. Why?

I had become addicted to opening more and more doors. Saying *no* wasn't part of my skill set. Having a lot going on felt good. I wore my open doors as a badge of honor showing that I was important, valued, and needed.

When a new door appeared, I seized the opportunity, and kicked it open. The reality was that keeping these doors open was hurting our business, damaging key relationships, and taking a toll on me. I wasn't giving anything my absolute best and I was losing ground on many fronts:

- My marriage was seriously strained. Jamie and I spent little time talking about anything more than our kids, schedules, employees, and the tasks we needed to complete just to keep things moving.
- My team members weren't getting the support and development that they needed from me. I was blowing in and out of the office for client meetings with little time to have real conversations with anyone.
- My kids were suffering from an absentee parent who missed far too many dinners, sporting events, and school gatherings.
- I was suffering physically, mentally, and emotionally. I wasn't sleeping enough and most meals were hurried and unhealthy.

Something had to give. Doors needed to close. I knew it intellectually, but found it emotionally difficult to close a few doors.

Then, everything changed. It was a Friday afternoon, and I had rushed back to Louisville from a trip out of town and met Jamie at an event. A client had just been promoted and his organization was holding a small party in his honor. I was supposed to pick Jamie up at our house so we could drive to the event together, but my flight was delayed. So, per usual, Jamie had driven there on her own to arrive at the start of the party. I flew into the airport, jumped into my car, and raced to the event. I was late. After the event, we drove home in separate cars. I stopped to get gas because I was nearly out of fuel. Out of nowhere, a storm appeared and the sky opened up, producing sheets of rain blowing sideways. It was unreal and caught me completely by surprise. In less than thirty seconds, I was soaked from head to toe.

Waterlogged from the unexpected storm, I pulled my car into the garage and grabbed my luggage from the back. I looked up to see Jamie standing at the top of the short set of steps that led to the doorway of our house. She was waiting for me and I could tell that she had something serious to share. I won't go into the details of our conversation that day, but many of you can imagine that the exchange was difficult and sobering. Much like my ride home from the event, I was out of gas and caught in the middle of an unrelenting storm.

What followed over the course of the next several weeks and months was tough. I did a fair amount of soul searching, trying to determine how I had messed up and what I needed to do to get back on track. I chose to deliberately close a few doors and invest time in understanding my purpose. Up until that day, I found it difficult to say *no* to things because I didn't want to disappoint others. In reality I was already disappointing plenty of people, but I was unable or unwilling to see it. Shutting the doors was tough, even though I wanted to do it. I still found myself hedging and looking for ways to keep some of them open a little bit.

In hindsight, it has been a wonderful journey. Do I still metaphorically run out of gas or get caught in an unexpected storm? Yes, but far less often. I tend to pay better attention to the gas gauge and check the weather forecast more often. I found that the better I get at it, the more I'm able to manage others' expectations and give my attention to what is most important. For me, closing doors allowed me to focus in certain areas, and those areas have grown. I finished my doctorate, we sold our company two years later, and I took a position at a great university. I also continue to consult with clients and grow another business. Our two kids are grown and both live near us in Nashville.

I don't know what doors might be before me, but for today, the tank is full and the sun is shining.

As you work to live out your purpose as a leader and to make a unique contribution, you and those around you will benefit from you making the decision to close a few doors. Identify which doors can close, and when the timing is right—do it.

DAY 13: CLOSE DOORS

Today's Thought

I had confused burning bridges with shutting doors. One is toxic and destructive. The other is liberating and, when done well, relationship- and career-enhancing.

Today's Questions

1. How difficult do you find it to close doors, turn off opportunities, or say *no* to something? Why do you think you answered that way?

   _____

   _____

2. What was the last door you left open too long or closed too quickly?

   _____

   _____

3. What would have happened if you had shut it a bit faster or kept it open a moment longer?

   _____

   _____

Today's Challenge

Identify a door that needs to close and start the process of closing it today.

DAY 14

GO ALL IN

Several summers ago, my family and I were visiting friends in Denmark. We were staying in a small coastal town in the northern part of the country. Throughout the town, store windows were peppered with signs announcing the annual visit from a troupe of traveling performers. The signs were not limited to our quaint village. Each adjacent town had signs announcing when the show was coming to their community.

We were intrigued. Having never been to a traveling Danish show before, we inquired about going and a group of us decided to take in the performance.

Denmark is a fairly small country with a population and geographic footprint comparable to North Carolina in the United States. Visitors are typically greeted with waving Danish flags and a stoic nod. Danes value how things are designed and work to make their homes cozy. They call it *hygge* (pronounced *hue-guh*). Hygge doesn't translate well in English. It is kind of like warm and cozy, but with a bit more of a Scandinavian flair. You almost have to experience it.

In short, Danes do things a certain way—the Danish way.

The troupe turned out to be surprisingly impressive. Every day, the show would travel from town to town. It had done so for generations. Because it employed so few people, everyone needed to perform, sell concessions, drive a truck, and erect the tent. It was an all-hands-on-deck type of experience.

The night of the performance, I walked into the arena and took a seat in the middle of the long row. I told Jamie, "If I sit on the aisle, there's a chance someone will grab me and make me participate in some way. So, I'm burying myself in the middle."

True, there were a few hundred people in the room, but I was convinced that I would be targeted for attention as one of a few non-locals in the place. I was not going to allow myself to be pulled into the performance.

Within minutes, a performer entered the arena and began interacting with the crowd. Sporting a large hat, he asked patrons to throw the hat from their seat in an attempt to land it on his head.

Like a magnet, he came to me. He extended his arm and handed me the hat. I threw it and missed. He made a face, the crowd laughed, and he moved on. Not too bad I thought—I was safe.

Twenty minutes later, the man was back. This time, he invited me to come onto the stage. I hesitated, even protested a bit. My mind was racing with questions:

- Why would I give up the comfort of my current position?
- There is a good likelihood that he is going to ask me to do something uncomfortable; what good could come from that?
- If this doesn't go well, it could be embarrassing. Who wants to face ridicule?

With the crowd's encouragement, I found myself moving toward the center of the tent.

Another audience member was invited to join me onstage. In everything we were asked to do, she was praised for her excellent performance and I was found to be less than stellar. The cast member poked fun at me and the audience laughed.

At some point, I flipped a switch in mind. I went from trying to fight the experience to wholeheartedly embracing it.

Here are some benefits I gained from throwing the switch and going all in:

- Being all in made the experience richer. I was an active part in creating something. Sure, the crowd was laughing, but I was having fun, too.
- The memories run so much deeper because I was all in. Instead of having a scant remembrance of the night, I can conjure up the entire evening in my mind. Yes, there is a video of my 'performance' to keep the memory fresh.

In today's world, it can be easy to be only partially present, somewhat engaged, or hedging our bets. I'll go a step farther and say that we are encouraged and rewarded for this type of behavior.

We are provided countless opportunities to:

- Put our resumes online and have them seeking new employment for us even as we sit in a meeting at our current workplace.
- Get a side hustle going to make a little money beyond our normal income to give us more options.
- Carry a device with us that we can use to escape the moment through access to thousands of apps.
- Flip through television channels, radio stations, and streaming service playlists looking for something a bit better to entertain us.

At some point, all this hustling, hedging, escaping, and flipping can cause us to miss out on something interesting, something that could make all the difference, change the game, or bend our trajectory. These options create limitless opportunities, but may also limit us from going all in.

For many of us, being risk-adverse or looking to avoid failure (even small failures) adds to the dilemma. Assuming we might fail at one thing, we may do a mediocre job at many things. So, we reduce risk of failure by choosing not to go all in.

As we age, our desire for comfort and control may even conspire against our willingness to take risks. Consider the last time you saw families at a swimming pool. Odds are that the kids were swimming and the adults were watching from the side. Kids are typically all in.

If you want to be a leader who makes a difference, delivers results that truly matter, impacts the lives of those around you, and builds a meaningful legacy, you must go all in. Don't wait any longer. The water is fine. Jump in and make some noise.

DAY 14: GO ALL IN

Today's Thought

If you are going to live out your purpose as a leader and make a unique contribution, you are going to have to make the conscious decision to go all in. Halfway isn't good enough.

Today's Questions

1. Are you more likely to jump all in on something, stand back and watch it play out, or do you fall somewhere in between?

    _____

    _____

2. What was the last thing you went all in on at work or school? How did it turn out?

    _____

    _____

3. What is something right now that you are hedging your bets about? What might happen if you go all in?

    _____

    _____

Today's Challenge

Have a conversation with someone you believe tends to go all in on things. Ask the person to describe what drives that type of full commitment behavior.

WEEK 2 WRAP-UP

T his week, you explored the importance of purpose and had a chance to consider the key components of leading others. This week's Application Worksheet is designed to help you draft your Leadership Impact Statement. This statement will help you better understand why you lead and provide you with a way of expressing your purpose to others.

1. Whom do serve in your role as a leader?

   _____

2. What results do those you serve want to achieve?

   _____

3. What barriers are impeding progress for those you serve?

   _____

4. What talents do you possess as a leader?

   _____

5. What is your inner voice or conscience telling you to do?

   _____

6. What are you passionate about?

   _____

7.   How do you want to be remembered as a leader?

_____

Use your answers to the previous questions to draft your Leadership Impact Statement.

Leadership Impact Statement

As a leader, I serve _____

(question #1) and assist in their efforts to _____

_____ (question #2). In doing so, I will help them to overcome barriers

including _____ (question #3)

by applying my talent for _____

__ (question #4), listening to my inner voice that encourages me to _____

_____ (question #5), and putting to use my

passion for _____ (question #6).

I choose to be remembered as a leader who _____

_____ (question #7).

DETERMINE PRIORITIES

The single sheet of easel paper hanging on the wall may have been easily discarded by a passerby as merely a few bullets scribbled in haste, but to those in the room it signified a huge victory. "All right," I said, "let's just do one last check-in before we wrap up our efforts for the day. Who agrees that these are the team's top two priorities?" All thirteen people raised their hands in agreement. For dramatic effect I added, "Does anyone oppose?" The room's response: silence.

The group's leader, Liam, stood up, moved next to me at the front of the room, and conveyed his gratitude to the group. "I know that this has been a long day, on top of a challenging few weeks, but I think we can all agree that we landed in a very good place." By all indications, everyone in the room concurred with his sentiments. Liam continued, "I want to personally thank all of you for your willingness to share your thoughts and for coming to today's discussion with a cooperative attitude. I feel really good about where we are going to take this organization, together."

To understand why the two items listed on the sheet mattered so much and to appreciate how getting everyone to agree to them was so remarkable, you need to understand a bit more of the story.

It was a cool April morning some three weeks earlier when, as I was arriving on campus for class, my phone rang. The caller introduced himself as Liam, explaining that a mutual friend had recommended that he give me a call to see if I would be willing to assist him with a challenge he was facing.

Liam shared that he was the division president of a tech company based in Chicago and that his company had recently acquired a startup in Ireland. The new startup was going to become part of his existing team. According to Liam, the integration of his existing Chicago team with the new Ireland-based employees was "a little bumpy at present." He informed me that his first attempt at bringing the group together ended in a meltdown, with one person storming out of the room after a tense discussion about email systems and two others engaging in a shouting match about staffing numbers.

"I knew there would be some apprehension about bringing the two teams together," Liam said. "I know that people are concerned about job security, are worried about how we will organize the teams going forward, and are wondering who will get which client accounts. I just didn't think it was going to be that bad. These are well-paid professionals, several of whom acted like children."

Liam explained that he had talked one-on-one with most of them since that contentious meeting, explaining that, going forward, that type of behavior wouldn't be tolerated and that he would appreciate them coming to the next meeting with a more open mind and commitment to figuring things out together. He then added that as poorly as they behaved, he knew that he was responsible for much of the problem. His attempt to function as the group's leader and the meeting facilitator simply didn't work.

"I believe that everyone, but especially the team members from Ireland, thought I was trying to drive the discussion to a particular outcome, but I wasn't. I was hoping that we would just get together, meet one another, and start acting like a team. I thought that sharing our CEO's vision for the company would be enough to galvanize us, but it wasn't. Instead, we ended up arguing about silly things." Liam explained that he felt it would be better for the next meeting to have an objective third party like myself in the room to direct the conversation. That would allow him to assume a seat at the table, as opposed to standing up front.

We talked a bit more about his expectations for the upcoming meeting and he responded, "I just want things to go better than last time." When I probed as to what better looked like, he didn't have a clear picture of how he wanted the day to transpire. Frankly, I think he was still a bit shell-shocked by the meltdown, was feeling the pressure from his boss, and wanted to avoid another bad meeting at all costs.

"Might I make a suggestion?" I asked.

"Please," Liam responded.

"What if we focus our energy on trying to agree to a couple of key priorities for the newly formed team? Nothing too overwhelming, just two or three priorities for the remainder of the year that everyone can agree to," I said.

"I'm listening," Liam added.

"It's been my experience that when people work to identify a few key priorities that they can tackle together, the discussion is often much more about what they can accomplish as a team than it is about arguing as to how they will do things," I continued. "You said that they were disagreeing about staffing numbers and email systems—those are *how* issues, not *what* issues. How is meaningless without what. Let's see if they can't identify a few key goals for themselves that align with the organization's strategy."

He agreed, and that's what we did. I'll spare you the details about how we pulled it off other than to say that from my experience whenever you bring a group of people together and work with them to set a few key priorities, it always has a positive impact on morale and commitment. Moving from discussions of a nebulous strategy or arguments about smaller issues to something tangible is time well spent.

This week is designed to help you do just that, by taking you from the broad thinking about your leadership purpose to specific priorities. To that end, you will spend each day learning about how to effectively set priorities. By the week's end, you will have identified two to three specific priorities that—when accomplished—will move you closer to your long-term goals.

**DAY
15**

RECOGNIZE STRATEGY

I n a three-day period, I heard three different people, in three very different settings, say nearly the exact same thing.

The first came when I was at a friend's house for dinner. There were several people at the gathering whom I didn't know. I struck up a conversation with an unfamiliar face and, during the course of our discussion, she asked me what I did for a living. After telling her that I taught strategy and marketing at Vanderbilt University, she responded, "Strategy, I love strategy. I've been told my entire life that I'm a strategic thinker." The expression on her face suggested that she agreed with the assessment others had shared with her.

The second incident came from a student who was signed up for my strategy classes. He visited my office at the beginning of the semester to introduce himself. We chatted for a few minutes about the objectives of the class, what the semester would entail, and what he hoped he would learn from the experience. As we wrapped up our brief chat and he headed toward the door, he glanced back and said, "I'm so glad that I'm signed up for this class, because I've always seen myself as a big-picture thinker."

The third episode in as many days occurred when I was talking to a client on the phone. He was discussing a goal that he and his team were working to achieve. When I inquired as to how the team was going to make it happen, he said, "I haven't worked out the details yet, but you know me, I'm more of the strategic type." When I asked further about his statement, he said that he likes to dream up things and leaves the dirty work of getting things done to others.

The word *strategy* is often bantered about in meetings, classrooms, cocktail parties, and everywhere else. Perhaps you've heard people express similar sentiments, saying things like:

- "I'm a strategic thinker."
- "We are shifting strategies right now."
- "Our strategy this year (or month) is . . ."

In many instances, the individual, team, or organization isn't truly pursuing a strategy or thinking strategically. They are exhibiting what I would consider to be more of a herd mentality. Similar to a herd of cattle, they are moving along with others—the market, competitors, etc.—as opposed to striking out in a new direction. Please hear me on this. Sometimes the herd mentality is effective and appropriate. Many organizations (dare I say most) follow this approach to varying degrees of success. But strategy is different. Done well, strategy is bold, and arguably brazen. It's bucking convention or reshaping how we collectively see things. It is about doing something sizably different, making trade-offs, and charting a new course. These behaviors are the essence of strategy, not the essence of the herd.

Now, I'm no cow expert but I do have some familiarity with the four-legged creatures. My in-laws own a small farm. In one of my first trips to their home, I sat and watched the cows grazing in the fields. It was interesting. Having grown up in the city, my bovine knowledge was limited to what I witnessed on television or saw whizzing by my car window as I drove down the interstate. Since my first farm visit, I have spent a fair amount of time watching cows in action. A literal sense of *in action* may be a bit of a misnomer. They aren't running wind sprints in the fields, but they do move around a fair amount wandering from the woods to the pond to the shelter to the pasture and back around to the woods. However, all of their progress is confined within the predesignated boundaries of the field. Occasionally, one cow breaks free from the herd, going off in a new direction; but it doesn't take long until the rest of the cattle catch up with the renegade herd member. I imagine that in their cow brains, they might feel like they are making progress, but the reality is that they are going in circles doing what is familiar and safe.

The same is true for many people when they set priorities for themselves. They tackle things that are familiar and safe. They are often merely going in circles.

Perhaps this has been the case for you, but my hope is that you will chart a new course for yourself. After all, you are working to be an inspired leader. You are reading this book and completing the steps to become the leader you want to be. I encourage you to use the time this week not to follow the herd mentality by looking to make incremental improvements in the priorities you set for yourself, but to set priorities that are bold and will take you to some new places. Challenge yourself to be truly strategic this week. Stick with me as we use our time together to seek greener pastures.

Use today to think about how you have historically approached establishing your priorities. Consider if you have used more of a strategic approach or a herd-like style.

DAY 15: RECOGNIZE STRATEGY

Today's Thought

Establishing strategic priorities may cause you to say *no* to many good, herd-following ideas, but these choices are what separate the very best leaders from the rest of the herd.

Today's Questions

1. How would you describe what it means to think strategically?

    _____

    _____

2. What limitations exist in your current role that keep you from being more strategic? Are you certain that those limitations exist, or are you merely assuming they exist?

    _____

    _____

3. As a leader, do you see yourself as more of a bold strategist or a herd follower? Are you okay with that position?

    _____

    _____

Today's Challenge

Write down some of the priorities you've set for yourself and accomplished over the last couple of years. Annotate whether each priority was a bold strategic move or a herdlike goal. For the ones that were following the herd, ask yourself how you could have been a bit more strategic.

AVOID ADDICTIONS

Many years ago, I worked for a leader who struggled with time management and prioritization. He would have us moving in one direction on Monday, another on Tuesday, and reverse course again by Thursday. The cumulative effect of his behavior was frustrating to the entire team. Everyone was exhausted; but it wasn't the type of exhaustion that stems from working numerous hours while accomplishing amazing things. We were exhausted from working many hours and feeling like we didn't get much done at all. Morale was in the tank.

The first kind of exhaustion is tiring, but fulfilling. The second one is tiring and demoralizing.

Nearly every night, the same question ran through my mind. I knew that I was really busy that day, but what had I accomplished that really mattered?

I rarely had a good answer.

A big portion of my frustration stemmed from the project sponsor. He was a genuinely nice man and I enjoyed his company. Nonetheless, our entire team was suffering under his leadership. He had the habit of changing his mind and shifting priorities nearly every day. My colleagues and I would spend half the day discussing priorities with the leader before coming to an agreement on the direction we would take. Then, the very next day, we would find ourselves back in the same meeting room having the exact same discussion all over again. One thing that I found particularly frustrating was that a hot issue on Monday that required everyone's attention was forgotten by Wednesday, as another urgent issue trumped our collective energies. The amount of time, resources, and effort expended for very little return was out of control and quite frustrating.

Over the years, I have found that many leaders who are operating with the best of intentions can cause all sorts of havoc for their people when it comes to setting and accomplishing priorities. Arguably, much of this priority-induced havoc stems from one of five addictions that you should avoid as a leader.

Allow me to share each of the five addictions.

1. ADDICTED TO NEW AND SHINY

Some leaders have never met an idea that they didn't like. Consider these examples:

- The leader reads the latest book and suddenly the entire organization is having a big taste of the flavor of the month. Priorities are shifting in yet another direction.
- The leader holds a meeting and a dozen new priorities, all of which require work, are launched simply because they were brought up in the discussion.
- The leader attends a conference and the buzzwords presented at the event become temporarily infused in her daily language. Suddenly she's rewriting everything to change to the new language.

Don't get me wrong. I'm not saying that leaders shouldn't learn new things. Of course they should! After all, you are working your way through a 5 Week Leadership Challenge and I'm asking you to try many new things.

What I'm saying is that leaders can become addicted to chasing the newest and shiniest ideas. Sometimes implementing a new idea makes perfect sense as the organization is ready to turn the page and take on a new approach, or a new concept is needed to catalyze the group to get something done. However, many times, a leader becomes infatuated with the new and shiny just because it is new and shiny, and the leader fails to consider the team's current situation.

A new idea or solution is of no value if it doesn't solve a specific problem. Your people simply become tired of chasing the latest great idea.

2. ADDICTED TO URGENCY

Some of us love urgency. We love putting out fires. It makes us feel useful, needed, and perhaps a bit important. Many leaders are the same way, and if they haven't paid the price to truly determine what is most important, they will spend their day racing from meeting to meeting or issue to issue without really assessing the relative importance of each situation.

What's the result? They are busy, but unproductive. Yes, they've filled the day, but they (and their people) feel unfulfilled.

3. ADDICTED TO ROUTINE

My grandfather delivered milk in Chicago. Every day, he traveled the same route through the city's streets. I imagine that he was up early every morning following a well-worn path. He likely could navigate his route from memory. It was routine—it was comfortable. This works well for milk delivery, but not necessarily for team or organizational growth. Leaders should look at their days to see if they have fallen into the delivery route trap. Unlike *addicted to new and shiny*, they may have become so complacent that they've created a milk delivery person culture. Perhaps a new routine, a new priority, or a new challenge is needed.

4. ADDICTED TO ACTIVITY

Have you ever sat in a meeting where each person reports to the boss about what they are working on, but no one talks about what they've actually accomplished? One by one, the attendees report on the activities they are performing. Each subsequent presenter spends a bit more time talking to demonstrate how busy he is.

The leader seems pleased. After all, everyone is so busy; there's a lot going on. Week after week, they have the same discussions with rarely anyone discussing where all the activity is getting the team, which priorities are being accomplished, or what results have been achieved. Leaders need to remember that organizations don't exist to simply do things. They exist to deliver results. Some leaders get these two confused. They aren't the same thing.

The game isn't to create the longest possible "to-do" list and check as much stuff off as possible.

The game is to win on a priority that really matters.

5. ADDICTED TO TALKING

Some leaders love to hear themselves talk. They hold meetings and do the majority of the talking. They conduct one-on-one performance reviews and dominate the conversation.

The problem with talking too much is that you often learn next to nothing.

If a leader wants to tap into an employee's passion, then the leader must learn how to ask good questions and listen with the intent of understanding, not with the intent of responding.

Understanding and tapping into an employee's passions is what allows employees to work crazy hard, be completely exhausted, and yet not be demoralized.

As you think about setting priorities this week and in the future, beware of these five addictions and do your best to avoid them. Today's thought, questions, and challenge are a great starting point.

DAY 16: AVOID ADDICTIONS

Today's Thought

Establishing priorities that matter and working diligently to accomplish them is an amazing source of energy and pride. It also feeds your sense of accomplishment.

Today's Questions

1. When was the last time that you left work feeling exhausted but fulfilled? What was the source of the fulfillment?

   _____

   _____

2. Think of a leader in your life who exhibited one of the five addictions. What was the situation and how did working for that leader make you feel?

   _____

   _____

3. How would you describe the difference between your answer to questions one and two?

   _____

   _____

Today's Challenge

Determine which of these five addictions you are most susceptible to and identify one or two actions that you can employ to avoid falling prey to that addiction in the future.

DAY
17

CHOOSE WISELY

I t was a perfect Saturday morning in late November. The weather was gorgeous. Not too warm or cold and the sun was shining. I took an early morning jog with my dog, followed by a walk with Jamie. We then enjoyed a leisurely brunch at a local restaurant and a bit of shopping in our neighborhood. It was delightful.

After strolling through a few stores, we found ourselves in the holiday spirit and decided to do a bit of decorating. We returned home and threw ourselves into the effort. I moved the boxes stuffed with holiday decorations from the garage into the house, we turned on the holiday music, and we started to transform the living room.

After a quick lunch in the kitchen, we switched our efforts to decorating the outside of our home. There was a large ceramic pot holding a once-beautiful plant. The plant had seen better days, so we decided to remove the dead vegetation and repurpose the pot by transporting it from the back of the house to the front porch as part of the holiday makeover. This pot was good sized, made of ceramic, and full of dirt. It weighed over eighty pounds (thirty-six kilograms).

As I set out to move the pot, I made four bad choices in a row that broke our great day.

1. **Forgetting that sometimes slow is fast.** In my haste to move the pot, I decided that carrying it would be faster than getting a cart from the garage.

2. **Putting ego over vulnerability and collaboration.** As I picked up the pot, I thought that I should get help, but my ego told me otherwise.

3. **Racing through yellow lights.** Deciding to cut through the house, I found the pot starting to slip in my hands. I elected to speed up and race toward the door as opposed to setting it down and adjusting my grip.

4. **Doubling down on a losing proposition.** When I reached the front door, my foot caught the threshold. Fearful of dropping and breaking the pot, I doubled down on a bad situation and attempted to keep the already falling pot from hitting the floor.

Good news: the pot didn't break.

Bad news: the pot hit my leg and the lower portion of my tibia snapped into two pieces.

Sure, breaking my leg was an accident. I didn't mean to drop the pot and break my leg. But the accident stemmed from four bad choices. I spent the remainder of the afternoon at urgent care. Until the new year, I found myself with plenty of unexpected downtime on the couch. The periods of stillness allowed me to assess what went wrong that late-November day. I considered how common it is for many of us to make similarly bad choices as we work to lead others. Odds are that people in your organization—perhaps you—are making similarly bad choices. Consider how these choices are showing up in your world.

FORGETTING THAT SLOW IS SOMETIMES FAST

Leaders and organizations like speed. They reward it. They tell stories about it. Leaders applaud the employee who works faster than everyone else and encourage others to pick up their pace. Organizations that are the first movers in an industry often benefit from their speed to market. This causes other companies to rush products and services to market. In many instances speed does matter, but there are times when slowing down and getting things right will be far faster in the long run. Don't allow your impatience to break your ability to win in the long run.

PUTTING EGO OVER VULNERABILITY AND COLLABORATION

Despite all of the discussions about collaboration and synergy in the workplace, many people try to carry everything on their own backs and not ask for help. There are a number of reasons that drive this behavior—desire to be a hero, past requests for help that didn't go well, or fear of looking weak. Whatever the purpose, the ego of one person can negatively impact the growth and success of many in the organization. Trying to carry everything on your back can, and often will, break you.

RACING THROUGH YELLOW LIGHTS

What do most people seem to do when the streetlight turns yellow? They speed up. The same happens in organizations.

- A salesperson senses that a client is hesitant about a purchase. Instead of exploring the issue and potentially losing the business, he speeds through the yellow light and inks the contract. In the long run the solution is wrong, the client is unhappy, and the long-term relationship is damaged. The client-relationship breaks.
- A job candidate gives several signs that she isn't a good fit for the job, but the organization desperately needs to fill the position, so they ignore the yellow lights and offer the candidate the job. Weeks later, everyone is miserable about the hiring decision. The situation is destined for a bad breakup.

DOUBLING DOWN ON A LOSING PROPOSITION

Sometimes things should have never started in the first place. What once sounded like a great project idea has eroded into an endeavor that everyone knows needs to be stopped. However, the organization has invested so much time, energy, and emotion into the effort that no one wants to call it quits. So, the elephant in the room grows bigger and bigger. Eventually, the thirteen-foot-tall, fifteen-thousand-pound pachyderm goes on a rampage breaking lots of stuff in the office.

I would imagine that you have seen all four of these, to varying degrees, play out in your life. Perhaps you have even fallen prey to them. I can also imagine that you can see how these four bad choices can negatively impact your ability to set and accomplish your top priorities.

DAY 17: CHOOSE WISELY

Today's Thought

The space between making a bad choice or a good one is often traversed by slowing down, asking others for input, and setting your ego to the side.

Today's Questions

1. How have you seen one of these bad choices play out in your team or organization?

   _____

   _____

2. What was the impact of the bad choice that you listed above?

   _____

   _____

3. Which of the four bad choices discussed in today's reading are you most prone to making? Why?

   _____

   _____

Today's Challenge

Throughout the day, try to consciously assess why you make the choices you make. Doing so will help you to be more aware of your thinking, even in the smallest of ways.

Ask yourself questions like:

- Why did I choose those words in that moment?

- What prompted me to eat that food versus something else?

- Where am I putting my time and energy right now?

DAY 18

BE BORING

A U.S.-based manufacturing company with locations throughout Europe was conducting a strategy session in Leuven, Belgium. Perhaps you've been involved in one of these meetings. A facilitator is in the front of the room working to control the direction of the conversation, asking questions to enhance understanding, and ultimately helping the group to develop their priorities. It involves a fair amount of brainstorming, listening, arguing, and collaborating among participants, but when it's done well, everyone leaves the room with a clear understanding of the way ahead.

In this instance, the goal of the session was for the leaders in the room to establish priorities for the next twenty-four to thirty-six months that would drive the broader organization's global strategy. As the CEO had told the group some weeks earlier, the key to the company's success going forward was to leverage the unique strengths of the European team and their position in the marketplace. General managers (GMs) from Italy, France, Germany, Belgium, and England were in the room. Each represented one of the five distinct product lines that the company produced. Historically, the GMs operated independently of one another, each with specific goals, budgets, and processes. Yes, they were part of one overarching company, but until that point they were connected in name only. Going forward, they were going to need to operate under a model the CEO was calling "One Europe" in which the GMs were expected to collaborate, cross-sell solutions, and partner in new ways to meet customer demands. When executed with excellence, the CEO said that they would go from five valuable, but independent product lines to one unstoppable force. The facilitator's goal that day was to get the five GMs to unify their efforts and commit to a few big One Europe priorities.

I was the session facilitator and I was having a difficult day.

Why?

When the company's CEO dispatched me, he told me to lead an "engaging session that would end in the creation of a strategy designed to reposition the company in the European market and fuel the company's global growth plan." That sounded like a great challenge and I was excited to play a role in making that happen.

Don't get me wrong, when I boarded the plane in the Unted States, I knew the event would stretch my facilitation skills as it is hard to get five minds to agree on something, especially when those minds had operated independently for years. However, the CEO had informed me that everyone was excited about the idea of creating a One Europe model. He said that my job was merely to help them to fill in the blanks with a few key goals. He made it sound easy.

Some forty-eight hours later, I was standing in a conference room, staring at an easel pad with a few lackluster ideas scribbled on it, surrounded by a room of people who were not willing to go big. Yes, they had heard the CEO talk about One Europe. They even nodded along with his argument for the move and verbally expressed their agreement. Now, faced with the need to commit, they were pulling back.

Allow me to hit pause in the story as there are numerous directions I could take the discussion. For our purpose, I want us to focus on the importance of being BORING when it comes to setting priorities.

By BORING, I mean:

Bold. Makes a strong proclamation

Optimistic. Focuses on what can be done

Radical. Pushes the status quo

Infectious. Creates buzz and interest

Needed. Works to solve a problem or provide a service that is needed

Galvanizing. Causes people to connect and bring their best

Here's what inspired my boring thinking.

In late 2016, Elon Musk announced a boring vision of his own. His idea was to combat the "soul-destroying traffic" in California with an underground tunnel system connecting the state's major cities. Musk called his new business The Boring Company and set out to bore under the SpaceX parking lot as a proof of concept. The company demonstrated the idea with the creation of the two-mile-long Hawthorne Tunnel. Now they are working to garner support from cities to implement a real-world application of the idea.

The goal of Musk's boring effort is to add a third alternative to ground transportation by allowing cars to travel below the surface using access points throughout the city. Some are excited by the idea. Others scoff at it. I can only imagine how people felt in the 1800s when a similar project was undertaken that eventually transformed how people in London commute. It took the boring vision of Charles Pearson over a hundred years to create what became the London Tube.

Now, back to the room of GMs who were unwilling to make big commitments. I asked the group a few boring questions. Things like:

- Imagine for a moment that One Europe works so well that every business news outlet in the world is scrambling to cover the story. What would the headlines read?
- If everything went perfectly, what outcomes could One Europe achieve?
- What status quo behaviors and processes would have to change?
- If we want to maximize employee excitement, what would need to be included in One Europe outcomes?
- What customer problems would we be able to solve that we haven't even considered addressing to this point?
- What would we learn individually and as a group if we could pull this off?
- If it were illegal for us to not succeed with One Europe (i.e., we'd all go to jail if we failed), what would we do?

These questions and others allowed the leaders to move past how things had been done and challenged them to create boring priorities of their own.

You may not be facilitating a strategic planning workshop in Europe or attempting to reconfigure the transportation infrastructure in your community, but it doesn't mean that you can't attack a boring effort of your own.

DAY 18: BE BORING

Today's Thought

Some of the best priorities you will ever set for yourself and create with others will be BORING:

Bold. Makes a strong proclamation
Optimistic. Focuses on what can be done
Radical. Pushes the status quo
Infectious. Creates buzz and interest
Needed. Works to solve a problem or provide a service that is needed
Galvanizing. Causes people to connect and bring their best

Today's Questions

1. At a high level, describe what a BORING priority could be for you?

    _____

    _____

2. Staying at that high level, why do you want to accomplish these things? What will they allow you to do? How do they connect to last week's purpose?

    _____

    _____

3. In looking at what you just wrote down, is it *bold*, *optimistic*, *radical*, *infectious*, *needed*, and *galvanizing*?

    _____

    _____

Today's Challenge

Connect with someone who you believe has set and accomplished a BORING priority, one that satisfies the six items in the acrostic. Ask the person who accomplished the BORING priority to describe the hardest thing they faced as they set out to be BORING.

At this point, you are a bit over the midway point in the challenge. I want to congratulate you for continuing to invest in yourself. My goal is to help you become a better leader. Taking the time to imagine what that looks like in your world can make all the difference.

DAY 19

ASK CUSTOMERS

You are likely familiar with one, if not several, of Marriott International's brands. With thirty-two offerings ranging from the high-end Ritz-Carlton and J. W. Marriott properties to the more affordable TownPlace Suites and Courtyard by Marriott, many of us don't have to travel too far to find a Marriott hotel. Today, Marriott is my company of choice when it comes to lodging, but that was not always the case.

Several years ago, I was asked to deliver a workshop for a client in Aruba. If you are ever asked to travel to Aruba for work, do it. The island was amazing and the people welcoming, but that's a story for another time. Today's lesson is not about visiting a tropical island. Instead, it's about something I learned leading up to the Aruba gig.

In preparation for my workshop, I was asked to observe a colleague delivering a similar session in Philadelphia, Pennsylvania. My colleague did a fabulous job leading the session and I learned a great deal from him; however, his facilitation, as great as it was, was not my biggest takeaway from the event.

For most of the day I sat next to David Marriott, the grandson of the company's founder, the current chief operating officer, and soon-to-be-chairman of Marriott International's board. At one point in the day, David and I struck up a conversation. Like most people in business meetings, our small talk focused primarily on our work. He provided a bit of a window into his day-to-day work and I reciprocated with a glance into my role. I shared with him that I travel a great deal for work and he asked, "Do you always stay at our hotels?"

With a bit of hesitation and embarrassment, I answered with an honest, "Always? No." I quickly added, "But, I do often stay at your properties." At that point in my career, I was traveling a lot. I probably stayed over two hundred nights per year in hotel rooms. Some were Marriott's rooms, but others belonged to their competitors.

While some business leaders might go on the defensive about why their company should always be the right choice or go on the attack and degrade the competition, David did neither. Instead, he thanked me for my business and then inquired, "Would you consider giving us all, or at least most, of your business in the future?" It was the perfect question, delivered with humility, confidence, and respect.

I instantly responded, "Yes, I could do that."

As I reflect on my response all of these years later, I think three things led me to provide an unequivocal *yes* to David's question:

1. There is little doubt that the source of the question had an impact on me. Denying that would be misleading. When a descendant of the founder and an executive of the company asks for your business, it's hard not to seriously consider it.

2. More important than the first issue, my decision stemmed from the reality that no one at any level of any lodging company had ever asked me for my business. Consider this. When I talked to David Marriott that day, I had spent thousands of nights in hotels and no one had ever asked for my continued business. Sure, I had received plenty of emails from a variety of establishments and I had several frequent traveler accounts for all the major hotel companies, but no one looked me in the eyes and simply asked for my business. I truly believe that as much as the source of the request mattered, it could have come from anyone and I would have very likely agreed. Why? I felt valued.

3. Lastly, if my experience at past Marriott hotels had been poor, I would not have complied with the request. I would have likely said, "Yes, I will consider doing that. Thank you for asking." I would have thought

about it and then decided to continue with my current practice in regard to lodging decisions. My point is that asking for a customer's business is key, but without a quality product or service, you will likely not garner a committed customer.

My conversation with David Marriott forever changed my relationship with the lodging company, but it goes much deeper than increasing the number of times I sleep in their hotels. I now provide feedback to Marriott, I spend more when I'm there, and I tell others to stay there, too. Why would I do these things? I want to see Marriott win because I know that when they win, I win; as their brand becomes better, my nights in their properties improve, as well.

The same is true for those you serve as a leader or those customers who use your products or services. They want to see you win because your success benefits them. So, make sure that you ask your employees and customers to help you to set priorities that truly matter. Ask for their input, listen to what they say, clarify to ensure you understand, and use what they provide to inform your thinking. Affording them a voice in the process is one way to ensure that the priorities you pick will align to those who matter most to you and your team.

DAY 19: ASK CUSTOMERS

Today's Thought

Investing time to ask your customers a few questions can yield insights that you will never gain on your own, no matter how smart you are.

Today's Questions

1. Of those you serve as a leader, who do you believe would be able to provide you valuable insight into the priorities you set for yourself?

_____

_____

2. How could you get the feedback from the person or people you listed above? Write out the specific steps to make it happen.

_____

_____

Today's Challenge

Take a few minutes to search the internet for an example of an organization that improved dramatically because of an idea that one of their customers provided to them. Consider what you can learn from the story.

DAY 20

CREATE MOMENTUM

Allow me to share a few things with you about the U.S. Army's Ranger School. It's mentally and physically exhausting. Most people who say they want to go to Ranger School never get a chance to attend the course. Demand is higher than the supply of class seats and there are many obstacles that can get in a soldier's way. Suffice it to say, getting into Ranger School is easier said than done.

Of those who do get a spot in the course, many don't make it through the first day. The initial physical fitness assessment consisting of push-ups, sit-ups, chin-ups, and a run, coupled with the intensity of the Ranger instructors administering the test, causes some to go home without ever unpacking a bag. You might be able to complete seventy-five perfect push-ups and run like the wind at home, but when you are faced with an evaluator who decides that only one out of every three push-ups you complete is good enough and sends you on a run without telling you how far or fast to go, it can be a recipe for failure. That said, making it through the gauntlet of the first day is no guarantee that you will complete the course or even the first phase.

When I went to Ranger School, the training consisted of four phases over the course of sixty-eight days. Each phase lasted for roughly one-fourth of the duration of the course; they consisted of woods, desert, mountain, and swamps, respectively. Injury, failed leadership roles, poor peer evaluations (kind of like being voted off the island on *Survivor*), and myriad other problems—even death—can stop the most prepared soldier from earning the coveted Ranger Tab. Needless to say, four hours of sleep per night, one meal per day, and plenty of stress to go around only adds to the experience. Plus, they recycle lots of people as well. This means you are sent back to repeat a section that you failed to pass the first time, second time, third time, or more—you get the point. Some people spend the better part of a year in the school and never graduate.

I was fortunate and completed Ranger School on my first try. It took me the minimum sixty-eight days from start to finish. Good preparation, a supportive spouse, great buddies, and lots of luck—not necessarily in that order—helped me complete the course. Less than 50 percent of the people who made it through the physical fitness test on day one were standing on the graduation field a few months later.

Completing Ranger School was a big priority for me. I set my sights on it when I was eighteen years old and I graduated at age twenty-three. Over the course of a five-year period, I set and accomplished numerous priorities—smaller building blocks—each of which gave me momentum, fueled my confidence, and helped prepare me for the next goal. First, I attended basic training and advanced individual training as a young soldier. I went to airborne school in the summer between my sophomore and junior years of college, and finished my time at the university after commissioning as an infantry officer. Upon completing the Infantry Basic Course, I had to do something that I was fearful of my entire life. I learned how to swim! Knowing how to swim is a requirement of Ranger School, as successful candidates must pass a Combat Water Survival Test.

The truth is that no one goes from ground zero to Ranger School, and few ever make it without a bit of wind at their backs—especially the type of wind that stems from accomplishing previous priorities.

Here are a few more examples in my life, but I'm sure that you can think of many in your life, too, if you invest that time to reflect on the goals you've accomplished:

- When I hiked Kilimanjaro with my son, Clay, it wasn't the first mountain we climbed. Previous hikes gave us momentum. On our way to the 19,341-foot (5,895-meter) peak in Tanzania, we logged hundreds of miles in Colorado, Nevada, and along the Appalachian Trail.
- When the company that Jamie and I owned landed a large client, it wasn't our first win. Things started small with one client who gave us a

chance, followed by another willing to do the same. Each project win gave us momentum, expanded our team's capabilities, and fueled our desire and ability to tackle more.

- When my team launched a successful leadership development product, it wasn't our first effort. Previous launches with various degrees of success taught us much and gave us momentum.

The same can be true for you. When you set priorities, consider the power of momentum. You may want to make big changes in the world—and I hope that you do—but don't set out with the goal of changing everything this year. You will likely fail and give up. The road to success is riddled with people full of great ambition but no momentum to fuel their efforts when times get tough. Set a more attainable goal and win. Then, stretch yourself a bit more and win again. Then, repeat over and over. That's how great victories are achieved. It's the power of momentum in action.

DAY 20: CREATE MOMENTUM

Today's Thought

Winning begets winning. Momentum fuels everything.

Today's Questions

1. What is one of the biggest personal or professional priorities you have ever accomplished?

   _____

   _____

2. What priorities did you set and accomplish along the way to achieving the big priority?

   _____

   _____

3. How did each subsequent win build your confidence and commitment?

   _____

   _____

Today's Challenge

Think of someone you know who has accomplished a big priority. Ask that person to share their journey with you. Listen to see what goals they accomplished along the way that helped build momentum.

**DAY
21**

OWN THE ROOM

I once delivered a presentation on leadership at Iceland's National Government Day. It was my fourth work trip to Iceland. Each trip was fun and exciting, but nothing like this particular trip. The event took place at Harpa, Reykjavik's iconic concert hall and convention center, and served as a celebration of Iceland's hundred years of sovereignty. Approximately five hundred Icelandic leaders, from all facets of the country's government, attended the session. My job was to talk to them about the importance of organizational culture and the role that each of them plays as leaders in shaping it.

I was in Iceland working with a much smaller group of leaders about three weeks earlier. During that visit, I was asked if I would consider returning to the country to present at the hundred years of sovereignty event. It was an honor to be invited and I accepted on the spot. I moved a few things around on my calendar, booked my travel arrangements, and in what seemed like the blink of an eye I was back in Iceland getting ready for the big day. I arrived early to the Harpa on the morning of the presentation, ensured that my presentation slides worked properly, and received a quick tutorial on the microphone.

All was good. I was ready.

I settled into my seat about fifteen minutes before the event's start time. Moments later, Iceland's prime minister, Katrín Jakobsdóttir, entered the room and joined my table. As the program's start time approached, my new tablemate and I chatted.

The time we spent talking, coupled with her subsequent presentation, proved a great example of how you can own a room when you are clear on your priorities. Although I arrived that day with every intention of helping the audience with their leadership skills, I quickly became the student and the prime minister the teacher.

Here are four behaviors that I saw Prime Minister Jakobsdóttir exhibit. I would suggest that you consider putting them into practice when you want to own a room as you share your most important goals.

1. BE PRESENT

With all that was going on that day—a large crowd, a pending speech, a myriad of other pressures from her role—it would have been completely understandable if the prime minister was distracted, but she wasn't. She was present. I have found that the most engaging people I've ever met have the ability to talk to you as if you are the only person in the room. She did just that. She actively listened, asked good questions, maintained strong eye contact, and showed a genuine curiosity.

While other leaders have their heads buried in smartphones, a present leader stands out in the crowd.

2. BE PERSONABLE

Not only was the prime minister present, she was extremely personable. She asked me about my travels, thanked me for attending the event, and posed with me for a few pictures. Being clear on her priorities, even in the moment, allowed her to comfortably focus her energy on me.

The prime minister's ability to be present extended to her time onstage when the ease of her presentation, sense of humor, and genuineness broke down the barriers that can exist between a large crowd and a single speaker when everyone is in a cavernous room.

3. BE PREPARED

Just prior to the event, I saw her glance at her presentation notes, but it was clear from the moment that she took the stage that she knew the content. She had prepared. Glancing at her notes likely grounded her in the topic.

Even though her speech was in Icelandic—and I barely speak two words of the language—it was clear that she knew her stuff. The delivery was not one that lacked preparation and the audience appreciated it.

You can be as present and personable as you want, but if you don't invest time to do the hard preparation work, all of the goodwill you create is easily squandered.

4. BE PROFOUND

Admittedly, I had to rely on others to fill me in on this one.

Although I watched the entire speech with great interest, my lack of Icelandic language skills allowed me to understand very little. It took a friendly note from a colleague across the table to fill me in on the details of the prime minister's speech.

I learned that the comments focused on the many changes and constants that the country had experienced over a hundred years of sovereignty. Participants were challenged to reflect on how the culture had evolved over the century and asked what values Icelanders will embrace in the future.

Her comments caused others to think and reflect. Profoundness does that.

In case you are wondering, my presentation went well that day. The crowd was gracious and seemed genuinely pleased by what I shared. I felt good about my performance, but knew that I was a bit overshadowed by the presenter who went before me. I'm okay with that, because I learned a great deal that day about what it means to be present, personable, prepared, and profound. I've worked hard since then to put those lessons into practice in my life.

As you share your priorities with others, don't miss out on the opportunity to be present, personable, prepared, and profound. These qualities will allow your message to cut through the noise and to ensure that your audience sees your brilliance. I contend that Iceland's prime minister owned the room that day because she was confident in the priorities that she had established. You can do the same.

DAY 21: OWN THE ROOM

Today's Thought

Being a great leader with clear priorities transcends geography, translates in any language, and has nothing to do with your title.

Today's Questions

1. Of the four behaviors discussed in today's reading (present, prepared, personable, and profound), which comes most naturally to you and why?

   _____

   _____

2. Which of the four behaviors do you struggle with the most and why?

   _____

   _____

Today's Challenge

Pick a priority that you established for yourself before you started reading this book. Now, pretend that you are standing at the front of a room explaining the priority to a large group of people. As you envision your presentation, how well do you see yourself owning the room?

WEEK 3 WRAP-UP

Congratulations on completing Week 3. You are 60 percent of your way through the 5 Week Leadership Challenge. Now is the time to set your top leadership priorities by following the steps outlined in this week's wrap-up.

PART 1

Step 1: Brainstorm Possible Priorities

In the space below, brainstorm possible projects, initiatives, goals, and so on that you can accomplish as a leader within the next six to twelve months.

_____

_____

_____

_____

_____

Step 2: Narrow the List of Possible Priorities

Review the list and place a star next to the five or fewer items that you consider to be the most viable priorities.

PART 2

Reduce Your Possible Priorities to Three or Fewer

Follow the instructions in the table below in order to narrow your list of possible priorities. Place the possible priorities that you put a star next to on the previous page into this chart and score as indicated. Your goal is to determine which possible priorities are truly most important. Limit yourself to a maximum of three selected priorities.

Possible Priorities Evaluation Matrix

List the five possible priorities that you identified in your brainstorming list. Give each possible priority a score (1 to 5) in response to each question at the top of the columns. Add up the numbers by row to determine the score for each possible priority. Based on the scores, determine your top three priorities.

1	2	3	4	5
No		Maybe		Yes

EVALUATION CRITERIA

	Feasible	Measurable	Motivating	Clear	Aligned	
Possible Priorities	Can I get it done?	Can I tell if I've won?	Does it excite me?	Is it easy to understand?	Does it support my purpose?	Total
1	+	+	+	+	=	0
2	+	+	+	+	=	0
3	+	+	+	+	=	0
4	+	+	+	+	=	0
5	+	+	+	+	=	0

PART 3

Finalize Your Priorities

To finalize your exercise, draft a statement for those priorities that scored the highest on the previous page and provide a compelling *why* for each.

Draft Your Priority Statement

The best priorities are written using a simple format that explains where you currently are, where you would like to be, and when you would like to get there. You want to be as specific as possible. Let's use an example of a personal priority that most can easily understand. If you said that your highest scoring priority from the previous page was to lose weight, then in this step you would list how much you weigh now, what you want to weigh in the future, and by what date you want to reach the desired weight. Something like this:

Example: Reduce my weight from 185 pounds (84 kg) to 175 pounds (79 kg) by December 31.

Provide a Compelling Why

You may fall behind or times may get tough as you work to accomplish the priorities you set for yourself. A compelling *why* will help you to keep going. Craft a statement that will motivate you. You can also use your compelling *why* to explain to others why this priority matters in the event that you need their help or support.

Example: In recent years, I have put on a bit of weight as a result of working extra hours and grabbing too much food on the go. Frankly, I haven't felt my best as a result. My self-esteem has fallen a bit and I have less energy. I want to be able to play sports with my friends and go on walks with my family. Losing weight will help me do that. It will also help me to be more confident at work.

Complete one of these sheets for each of your priorities. Use the information and examples on the previous page as a guide.

Priority #1

_____ (current state)

to _____ (desired state)

by _____ (target date)

Your Compelling *Why*

Priority #2

_____ (current state)

to _____ (desired state)

by _____ (target date)

Your Compelling *Why*

Priority #3

_____ (current state)

to _____ (desired state)

by _____ (target date)

Your Compelling *Why*

CREATE
PLANS

Malaysia's capital, Kuala Lumpur, served as my family's temporary home for a couple of weeks while I worked there several years ago. Our hotel sat across the street from the famous Petronas Towers, known for the iconic bridge that spans the two buildings, and wonderful restaurants, parks, and shopping nearby. We enjoyed our time in the vibrant city and benefited greatly from its inhabitants.

From the time we arrived, Jamie planned the various activities that she and the kids would do during the day and what the four of us would do in the evenings when my workday wrapped up. She planned the meals, picked destinations to visit, and coordinated transportation to various locations throughout the city. She planned everything, with one exception. It was my job to determine how we would spend our one free Saturday in town.

Busy working, or at least that was my excuse, I delayed planning the outing until the very last minute. The Friday before our Saturday outing, I did a quick search of the internet in an attempt to find a suitable destination. Something caught my eye. A tourism website touted a former fort on a hill that offered a beautiful view of the area and the chance to see a few monkeys. It sounded good to me. So, I hired a driver for the day and shared my big plans with the family. Clay was on board at the mention of the monkeys. Alex and Jamie needed a bit more convincing but promises of an enjoyable car ride and the beautiful views convinced them that it would be fun.

The next morning, my plan started perfectly. We found the driver in front of our hotel as promised, sitting behind the wheel of a clean and tidy car. He jumped out of the front seat to open the door for Jamie as we approached. She smiled at me and I smiled back, confident that I had lucked my way into the perfect day.

We arrived at the base of the hill and our driver told us to wait while he purchased our tickets, explaining that he wasn't allowed to drive the car into the park. In all honesty, I was a little concerned in the moment thinking that we would have to walk to the top of the hill in the heat, but again luck prevailed and the driver returned with entrance passes and informed us that the tram should arrive soon. Ah, a tram, just as I planned. The tram arrived as advertised. It was cute, roomy, and filled with tourists just like us who were also excited to see the monkeys. As the tram departed the ticket booth, we waved goodbye to our driver who elected to wait by the car.

The tourist transport worked its way to the top of the hill. The closer we got to the summit, the greater the excitement. We rounded a corner near the crest of the hill and the trees gave way to our first glimpse of a wall that stood around the former fort. Perched at the top of the structure was a monkey sitting like a sentry on duty. People were ecstatic snapping photos and pointing at the primate looking down at them. Another monkey appeared, and then another and another. To say our tram was alive with delight was no exaggeration.

The road plateaued at the top of the hill and the tram stopped for all to disembark. As we stepped from the tram, there were at least five or six monkeys milling about. Two men stood next to carts on the far side of a small paved area. Each cart was covered in a variety of monkey snacks that were shielded from the sun by large umbrellas hovering above the stands. I offered to grab some monkey snacks and joined the line forming in front of the nearest of the two stands. As I waited my turn, I noticed that more monkeys were starting to arrive. Some attempted to steal items off the cart, but the crafty food vendors managed to disrupt their advances using a stick in one hand while continuing to exchange money with the other. When it was my turn, I stepped up to the cart and purchased a couple of items for my kids to give to the monkeys. With monkey food in hand, I spun around to head back to my family so we could distribute the goods to our new-found primate friends. That's when it happened. The three-foot-tall sweethearts roaming around me pounced. Suddenly they seemed much larger and much more aggressive. One monkey latched onto my front, standing on the waistband of my shorts and grabbing hold of my shirt. Two others began tugging at my arms. It was a full-on attack and I was not prepared for the onslaught as other monkeys, sensing weakness, advanced on my position. I dropped the food. They pounced on the booty and I scampered back to my family.

I would have been more embarrassed by my actions, but similar squabbles were breaking out all around me. Monkeys were springing from every direction, food was flying, and people were scrambling. What had been a gleeful crew of tram-riding adventurers a few minutes ago quickly turned into a panicked pack of tourists in well over their heads and longing to find the exit. At that point, there were probably twenty tourists, a hundred monkeys, and no tram. We hunkered down in small groups, standing back-to-back. The monkeys roamed about with complete freedom and confidence. They were in charge and they knew it. Things finally started to settle down. Food purchasing had stopped. The venders remained stoically by their carts. Most of the monkeys slipped back into the woodline. A good fifteen minutes passed.

Then we heard the grinding engine of the tram as it worked its way back to the top of the hill. As it rounded the bend, I started to make out the faces of the next batch of victims. They were excited, snapping photos, and pulling out their wallets in order to buy some treats for the cute monkeys. The group I came up with couldn't get back on the tram fast enough. Just to remind us that they were running the operation and to deliver one last scare, a few monkeys jumped on the tram with us. They were quickly shooed away by the tram driver, but we all got the message.

We made our way back down the hill and to our car. We asked the driver to take us back to Kuala Lumpur as we'd had enough adventure for the day. My outfit had gotten pretty dirty and we all felt in need of showers. Instead of the nice meal I had promised at the outset of the day, we settled for a quick bite from the shopping center across the street from our hotel.

Two days later over a cup of coffee, I told a colleague about the experience. He just laughed at me. "I know exactly where you went," he said. "That place is notorious for aggressive monkeys." He then rattled off a dozen other places that we should have gone to instead of visiting the monkeys on the hill. "You should have asked around. We would have helped you come up with a much better plan for how to spend the day."

In this instance, I had failed to plan. I waited until the last minute, made decisions without enough information, and asked no one for advice. I wish I could say that this was the first and last time I have ever done that, but that would be a lie. I'm a trained project manager with years of planning experience, yet on occasion I find myself failing to plan well. I would venture to say that you do the same at times. True, you may not have a monkey hanging from your front as I did, but poor planning may have hoisted a few proverbial monkeys onto your back.

This week you are going to explore the importance of planning. The daily activities will provide you the chance to consider various aspects of planning and to reflect on how you typically approach creating plans both on your own and with others. By the end of the week, you will have the chance to create plans for the priorities that you set last week.

One last thing. The stairwell in our house is lined with photos of our family over the years. There are pictures of weddings, graduations, and other momentous occasions. Grandparents, aunts, uncles, cousins, siblings, and good friends adorn the wall. The third picture from the left at the bottom of the stairs is one that my daughter, Alex, captured the moment I turned around after buying the monkey food. The look on my face is the perfect example of how one looks when they fail to plan well.

ENCOURAGE OWNERSHIP

Determining how you will accomplish your priorities allows you to begin to truly own the goals, as planning helps us move from the abstract to the tangible. The same is true when you bring others into the planning process. As your team members work to create plans, you will see different ideas emerge about how to do the work. You will watch team members question tasks and refine timelines. Most importantly, you will observe people moving from passive participants to active owners of the priorities.

I recently had a chance to see the power of this type of ownership in action.

As a faculty member at Vanderbilt University, I'm fortunate to work with students in a number of capacities both in and out of the classroom. Beginning in the 2018–2019 academic year, I was asked to serve as faculty advisor to an Innovation Garage (IG) team in Vanderbilt's Wond'ry. The Wond'ry is Vanderbilt's innovation center. It is a space for students, faculty, and staff to collaborate and bring ideas from concept to reality through the use of a wide range of Wond'ry-provided resources, programs, and events.

The Wond'ry's IG program allows students, faculty, staff, and an outside corporate sponsor to partner as they create a solution to a real-world problem. Over the course of an entire year running from August to August, IG teams perform a significant amount of research, analysis, business case development, and solution design, culminating with the creation of a minimal viable product (MVP) for the corporate sponsor. Students are challenged to stretch themselves as they deliver the presentation to corporate executives and operate under tight timelines. The experience is unique, intense, and rewarding.

With one year of IG experience under my belt, I was excited to start with a new IG team for the 2019–2020 academic year. It was late August in Nashville. The air was hot and humid. Fortunately, I was enjoying the air-conditioned comfort in one of the Wond'ry's conference rooms waiting for the kickoff meeting to start for my new IG team. The meeting's start time approached as the usual pleasantries and small talk filled the air. Slowly, everyone settled into their seats around the table. With six students, three faculty, and five representatives from the sponsoring company in attendance, the table was full. I watched as students met each other for the first time, introduced themselves to the company's executives, and interacted with Wond'ry leadership. At one point in the kickoff day, a few students from the previous year's IG team joined us. When the IG is in full swing, I typically attend two to three student meetings per week. The summer provides a slight hiatus from that routine. Students are working as interns with the corporate sponsor. As a result, faculty/student interaction slows. So, I was excited to catch up with last year's team members and learn what they had accomplished over the course of the summer. Believe it or not, last year's students had more on their minds than satisfying my personal need to catch up. They were charged with showcasing their work to the newest crop of IG participants by walking everyone through their project.

What stuck with me most that day was not hearing about what last year's students accomplished over the course of the year. I was already intimately familiar with their work. What stood out to me was how the students fully owned the project. After the meeting, I reflected on the students' ownership of the project and captured six amazing takeaways that came from this type of ownership. As you read through the six takeaways, remember that all of them started because the students owned the plan. They created it. They executed it.

1. OVERCOME OBSTACLES

Like any project team, the students ran into obstacles. Everything from scheduling conflicts to scope creep emerged throughout the course of their efforts. Because they owned the plan, they also owned dealing with the obstacles. Their creativity emerged and allowed them to go around, move out of the way, or tackle any obstacles that hindered progress.

2. PERSONAL GROWTH

The results that the students delivered were a function of individual contributions to creating a plan and accomplishing the team priority. The process allowed the team to grow collectively and team members to grow individually. In many instances, team members volunteered in areas that would require them to stretch.

3. FIND PURPOSE

As I worked with the students over the course of the project, I found that some discovered a passion for certain aspects of the effort. Owning the plan and the work allowed them to explore their own interests at a deeper level. This led to a better understanding of their purpose.

4. SHARE BURDEN

Let's not sugarcoat the situation. We've all worked with enough teams to know that burdens aren't always equally shared. At times one person carries the weight of the project on her shoulders and others evade most responsibility. That said, my work with the teams revealed an amazing amount of burden sharing. Because they had many other responsibilities on their plates and collectively owned the plan, they stepped up and willingly shared the burden.

5. DELIVER RESULTS

Overcoming obstacles, sharing burdens, and the like are all good things, but in the end, the team had to deliver results. And they did. Why? They owned things from start to finish. There was no handing off to another person to finish the work. Each team member stood up in front of the corporate sponsor and owned the results of the team's efforts.

6. BUILD PRIDE

As I watched the students over the course of the year, I saw people with their heads held high. They made it happen. They owned it. In turn, they had a sense of pride in what they accomplished. While being prideful can sometimes be negative, being proud of what the team has accomplished for their clients is a positive.

DAY 22: ENCOURAGE OWNERSHIP

Today's Thought

If you want people to own the results, they need to own the plan. Bringing team members into the discussion early creates a sense of ownership from the beginning.

Today's Questions

1. When you are creating a plan to accomplish a priority, how do you engage others in the planning processes?

    _____

    _____

2. Which of the six takeaways from today's reading have you personally experienced? How did this experience unfold?

    _____

    _____

3. What are the pros and cons of bringing team members into the planning process?

    _____

    _____

Today's Challenge

Reflect on a time when your leader acted independently of you and your team by creating both the priorities and the plan to accomplish them. Consider how it felt to be left out of the process.

SPUR IMAGINATION

had just closed my laptop and shifted my mind from work to dinner, when my daughter, Alex, entered the room. "I'm going to the hardware store; do you want to come with me?" she asked. Without hesitation, I answered, "Yes." I didn't ask why she wanted to go or what she wanted to get. I knew that information would come out soon enough. I just signed up for the trip and grabbed my keys because I've learned over time when Alex is wanting to go to the hardware store she has something creative in mind.

Most of my adventures with Alex involve helping her to breathe new life into old items or watching her create something new from scratch. I have watched Alex transform a broken chair, that most of us would discard, into a beautiful treasure fit for any home. I've also observed her taking a few, seemingly disparate ideas, and using them as the source of inspiration to create an original piece of art. On our Friday afternoon drive to the hardware store, I quickly learned that this trip fell into the latter category. Alex was imagining something new.

She told me about a decorating idea that she had come across on the internet and how that idea, fused with something she saw in a magazine, had inspired her to create a mural on a large piece of wood. Alex shared her idea with me in the car on the way to the store and filled in the details as we wandered through the lumber and paint aisles gathering supplies. The more she talked about the project, the greater her enthusiasm. Having traveled down similar paths with her in the past,

I knew that, although I couldn't fully grasp what she was envisioning, I should encourage her to do it. Experience had taught me that something amazing always comes out on the other side of her creative process.

When we arrived back at the house, she immediately went to work in the garage clearing a workspace, prepping materials, and sketching her design. She worked feverishly late into the night and was back at the task first thing in the morning. Less than twenty-four hours after asking me to go to the store with her, she invited the family into the garage to unveil her work. It was incredible. She had painted a gorgeous mural featuring a black-and-white abstract image that spanned three pieces of birchwood. I stood in awe as I looked at what she created out of a few random items from the hardware store. That piece of work now adorns a wall in her own home.

If you are reading this thinking that you lack Alex's artistic skills, don't worry. Today's lesson isn't about painting, drawing, sculpting, or sewing. Instead, the lesson is about an amazingly powerful word that Alex puts into practice in her artwork and that you and your team need to put to use in your endeavors.

What's the word? Stick with me for a moment.

Imagine that your organization has been struggling with an issue for a long, long time. Occasionally, the problem goes away; but it inevitably reappears. People are frustrated with this recurring and costly issue.

Can't think of a problem in your world? Allow me to jog your thinking with a few ideas:

- Perhaps your reoccurring issue is a technology solution that isn't working quite right. The organization has invested a lot of money to resolve the issue and people have spent countless hours troubleshooting the problem; however, it just doesn't work as promised.
- Maybe it is a performance issue that has yet to be resolved. At times, it seems under control and things are going well, then it flares up in unexpected ways.
- It could be a customer complaint that comes and goes. Customers have valid concerns, but despite meetings to discuss the source of the problem, your team can't determine the root cause.

Whatever the problem, it persists. Everyone is frustrated with it.

Now imagine that the next time the problem is discussed, you offer a sugges-tion. Your thought is unique. It causes people to pause. Discussion ensues and everyone agrees that your thought could work. It could change the game.

Imagine that six months later, people are reflecting on the day you made your suggestion and everything changed. What had once seemed impossible now is a non-issue. In fact, the organization is in a far better place because of your recom-mendation, and you are seen in a completely new light. You are the problem-solver. You are the catalyst of the idea that made all the difference. You are destined for amazing things.

Feeling pretty good, eh?

If so, you just felt the power of the one word that *must* be in your vocabulary. What's the word? *Imagine*.

Attempting to accomplish a priority that you haven't accomplished before takes creativity, innovation, and, yes, imagination.

Artists, creatives, and visionaries have been putting the art of imagination to work for years.

- John Lennon used it as the title of his 1971 album, *Imagine*, and the lead track from the record.
- Walt Disney famously said, "Laughter is timeless, imagination has no age, dreams are forever."
- Maya Angelou challenged our commitment to a peaceful world with, "If we live long enough, we may even get over war. I imagine a time when somebody will mention the word war and everyone in the room will start to laugh. And what do you mean war?"
- Nelson Mandela's words echoed the importance of the term. "Those who can't imagine change reveal the deficits of their imaginations, not the difficulty of change."

When you are working to put together a plan, challenge yourself and others to put imagination to work in order to create plans that will help you to accomplish your priorities. Ask questions like:

- Imagine if it were illegal for us to not solve the problem we are facing; what might we do?

- Imagine what performance might look like if every team member was so engaged that you had to force them to go at the end of the day; how might we create that sort of environment?
- Imagine if we had our customers' unwavering loyalty to the point where they openly cheered for us every day; what might we be able to achieve?

Some of these questions might feel a bit absurd, but if they caused you to pause and think differently, then they are doing the trick. The term *imagination* is truly a powerful one. In fact, take a moment and just imagine for yourself what it would be like if you became the leader you truly want to be. Imagine what your world looks like if you can be the leader your people deserve, if you can fulfill your purpose, if you can accomplish big priorities, and if you can put plans together that drive success.

DAY 23: SPUR IMAGINATION

Today's Thought

Leaders who frequently employ the word *imagine* when working with others foster a spirit of creativity, determination, and potential.

Today's Questions

1. When did you work to solve a problem where the solution proved to be truly unique or creative? How did that feel?

   _____

   _____

2. What challenges are you currently facing that you have been dealing with for far too long? What solutions have you tried so far?

   _____

   _____

Today's Challenge

Pick one of the challenges that you described in your response to the second question above. Think of someone who is familiar with the conversation and ask her this question: "Knowing what you know about the challenge I'm facing, imagine for a moment that it would be illegal for me to not solve the problem. What advice would you give me?"

UNDERSTAND RELATIONSHIPS

A s a project manager at KPMG Consulting, I found myself working with a wide range of stakeholders. The list seemed to get longer at nearly every turn and included my team members, our project sponsor, my direct manager, executives both in my firm and on the client side, and various subcontractors. The project I was working on was far-reaching and it seemed like every person I interacted with had an interest in the success of the project.

My innate desire to keep all of them happy was quickly becoming my downfall. I was arriving to work earlier each day and leaving later at night, yet I still felt like I was losing ground on my quest to please all. Not only was it physically exhausting to try to please everyone, but those who truly mattered most were suffering because they weren't getting the best of my attention as I was splitting my energy among too many competing interests.

When you are creating plans as a leader, it is important to listen to others and take their thoughts, ideas, and insights under consideration, but it is just as important to understand that not all relationships are created equal. Some relationships matter more than others when it comes to the results of your work, and some relationships matter more when it comes to generating those results.

At this point, you may be asking yourself, "What is he talking about? Of course, all people are created equal."

If that's your reaction, I invite you to reread what I wrote.

I am not saying that all people aren't created equal. They are. Every person has tremendous potential, capability, energy, excitement, and a wealth of attributes that makes each important, unique, and valuable. I'm simply saying that all *relationships* are not created equal and that when you are leading yourself and others through the planning process, you must understand which voices truly need to be engaged. These are the people that you need to talk to and with when you are creating a plan. These are the ones who need to help you brainstorm ideas and weigh options. These are the ones who will truly be needed when you begin to implement the plan. And these are ones who will ultimately judge your team's success.

Here are a few examples to consider as you think about this concept:

1. CLIENT RELATIONSHIPS

Many organizations find that the majority of their revenue comes from a minority of their clients. It is the 80/20 rule in action, with 80 percent of revenue consistently coming from 20 percent of clients. If this idea is directionally accurate in your world, then maintaining strong relationships with key clients matters more than attempting to spread yourself thin across all of your clients.

Great leaders understand this, identify the key client relationships, and invest time in cultivating relationships with the most important existing and potential clients. They understand the importance of listening to key clients to ensure their input is fully considered when creating plans. In turn, these leaders put systems in place to ensure that they remain connected to every key customer.

2. PARTNER RELATIONSHIPS

As a leader, you will likely have numerous partners regardless of your leadership role. These can be suppliers, distributors, logisticians, and many others. Arguably, each partner is important to the planning process, but only a few are critically important and require a leader's best attention. Here are a few possible examples:

- A key supplier who provides a crucial raw material that is time-sensitive or difficult to come by.

- A member of the logistics chain that is vital to delivering products to key customers on time.
- A distributor who sells to a critical geography that you can't reach without or who contributes a large sales volume compared to other distributors.

Great leaders take the time to consider all of the organization's partners and identify those that require the leader's finest energy and attention.

3. EMPLOYEE RELATIONSHIPS

If you work in human resources, the thought that some employee relationships matter more than other relationships may make you cringe, but hear me out on this one.

The existence of strong relationships among coworkers and between a leader and team members is very important. In fact, the breakdown of these relationships often leads to erosion in the organization's culture. A great leader gets this and works to create an environment where great relationships flourish and team members can trust one another.

However, a team leader doesn't see it as her job to have a great relationship with every employee in an organization. Nor does she see it as her job to get everyone's ideas into a plan. She understands that her job involves creating strong relationships with her direct reports and other key connections in the organization. These are the people who need to be involved when creating plans to accomplish priorities.

In a very real sense, relationships come and go in life. Situations change over time.

The point is that as you think about how you will accomplish the priorities you have set for yourself, or those that you have crafted with your team, it is critical to think about the relationships that you have in place right now. It is highly likely that some people can help you accomplish what you are setting out to do. It is equally likely that some people could help you but you have either a damaged or nonexistent relationship with them. Now is the time to strengthen the latter and fix the former.

It's also the time to ask others for help. If you have someone on your team who can fulfill a particular role, let them do it. If you have someone in your life who can give you good advice, go to them and ask for help. Think about the relationships you have in life and how you can work in concert with others to accomplish your top priorities. Time is too short and resources too limited to continue trying to please everyone or always be trying to make things happen on your own.

Now is the time to understand and leverage the power of relationships.

DAY 24: UNDERSTAND RELATIONSHIPS

Today's Thought

It is important to get input from others during the planning process, but what is even more important is ensuring the correct individuals are involved—because some ideas, insights, and perspectives are more critical than others.

Today's Questions

1. Which stakeholders truly matter and can offer you the best insights as a leader?

    _____

    _____

2. What should you do today to build stronger relationships with your top customers, employees, and partners who can provide you the best insights?

    _____

    _____

Today's Challenge

Reach out to one person who you believe is key to the success of one of your priorities. Ask that person to meet with you in the next two to three weeks to review the plans you are creating. Once you get someone to commit, put a date on the calendar within the next two to three weeks to have the conversation.

DAY 25

REMAIN OPEN

In 2019, professional golfer Tiger Woods did what many had thought he would never accomplish. He won the Masters Golf Tournament fourteen years after his last win at the Augusta National Golf Club and nearly ten years following a very public unraveling of his personal life. Like many, I watched portions of the tournament on television as turnaround stories always capture our collective attention. One thing I noticed was the amount of airtime that the golf commentators invested in discussing Tiger Woods's club choice. I learned that Woods had historically carried a Scott Cameron putter and exclusively played Nike irons; however, things had changed. Nike had moved away from producing golf clubs, and the Scott Cameron Putter that Woods traditionally carried didn't play too well for him during the previous golf season. So, new putters entered the bag, and irons produced by TaylorMade were now taking up a bigger spot on his club list.

Golf enthusiasts eat up this kind of information.

I'm not a golf enthusiast. My golf interest is limited to an outing every year or so with my dad and my two brothers. My oldest sibling and father take the game very seriously. My other brother and I are much more interested in driving golf carts and eating snacks. In fairness, we start our rounds with the best of intentions, but a bad shot off the first tee and four-putting at the end of hole one quickly deflate our enthusiasm. I spend most of my time going from one fairway to another, neither of which are the one I'm supposed to be on for the actual hole that I'm playing in the moment. By the third or fourth tee box, our minds drift to snack food.

So, why would I become interested in learning about what clubs Tiger Woods was carrying in the 2019 Masters Golf Tournament?

Well, my interest had nothing to do with the specific putters, irons, or any other club in his bag. I became intrigued because of his choice to change at all and the commentary I heard and later read on the subject.

A quick search of the internet that weekend revealed that some observers applauded Woods's decisions, saying that it was smart of him to make use of the best technology and to leverage any available tool to regain a position at the top of the leaderboard. Others chastised Woods and criticized his choices. They argued that Tiger Woods doesn't do what others do. He shouldn't start to carry the same clubs as other players. Tiger leads, he doesn't follow, they complained—adding that changing clubs is another sign of weakness in Woods's armor.

As I listened to the latter, I thought to myself, "Since when is trying something new, making use of technological advancements, learning from others, or changing one's mind a sign of weakness?"

My answer to the question: in the eyes of many, it is seen as a weakness all the time.

Consider these quick examples:

- A politician takes a position on an issue. When new information on the subject is learned, he changes his mind. People (especially opponents) don't call him enlightened or smart; they label him a flip-flopper.
- Your company starts a new project and puts energy and funding behind it. Six months into the effort, something changes. Perhaps the solution is no longer needed or a better option appears, yet the project continues. No one wants to admit the mistake or stop the train.
- You become comfortable in your job. You enjoy the routine. Nonetheless, a voice in your head says that it's time to move on, to try something different, or take a new direction. Yet, you do nothing. Perhaps you don't want to risk failure or are concerned that you will disappoint someone else.

Writing today's lesson caused me to think a bit more about the annual golf outings with my dad. True, he doesn't drive the ball like Tiger Woods. Yes, his chip shots and putts don't quite have Tiger's touch. But like the 2019 Masters Golf Tournament champion, my eighty-nine-year-old father continues to bring new clubs, techniques, and approaches to his golf game. In recent years, my dad has had both knees replaced. He purposely scheduled the surgery in the dead of winter so he would be ready to golf come spring. As a result, his golf swing looks like that of a person half his age.

When I think about my dad's golf game and his approach to the sport, I'm blown away. He continues to play golf two days a week, picks up new friends to play with, and takes on the challenge of adding golf courses to his routine. I stand in awe when he drops a twenty-five-foot (eight-meter) putt or chips the ball from seventy-five yards out to within inches of the hole. Did I mention that he worked two jobs most of my life and, together with my mom, raised five kids? He may have wanted to play golf when he was younger, but it wasn't much of an option for him. Sneaking away for five hours wasn't in the cards. So he didn't really play golf until later in life. In fact, his interest in the game has grown over the last few decades. Everything that my dad does on the golf course comes from a firm commitment to embracing the new.

Regardless of your situation and what you know and don't know about something, you should always be open to embracing the new. Being open to the new can change everything about how you lead others and the results that you achieve. It can also change everything for the people on your team. So, be willing to put a new golf club in your bag, change your swing, and hang out with a few new players. Who knows, you might learn a thing or two in the process.

DAY 25: REMAIN OPEN

Today's Thought

If you set out to accomplish priorities that you have never accomplished before, you need to remain open to new ways of doing things.

Today's Questions

1. When was the last time you set out to learn something new, find a better way to move forward, or take a step in a different direction? What happened?

    _____

    _____

2. How might something you are currently doing benefit from putting a new club in your golf bag?

    _____

    _____

Today's Challenge

What tool have you grown overly accustomed to using in your day-to-day work? Vow to put it down for two days in an effort to try something new instead.

LET GO

Early on in our business, Jamie and I decided that we wanted to intentionally build an organization of high trust, flexibility, and an entrepreneurial mindset. Ten years into our careers, we both had worked in organizations and around leaders where suspicion was the default position, rules were etched in stone even when they served no one well, and personal initiative and creativity seemed reserved for a select few people. Am I suggesting that we got all of it right? Nope. Far from it. But the intention was authentic and we worked to make it happen.

Like many leaders, we created mission and vision statements, crafted our strategy, and defined the organization's values. As our firm grew, we shared our thoughts on the importance of our culture and the role each and every employee played in bringing our vision to life. Over time, the vision became less our view on things and more of a collective vision that included the voices of many.

We welcomed this change for two main reasons. First, the input of our team members allowed Jamie and me the chance to better refine our vision. They challenged us to think in new ways and helped us to better see what was possible. Second, including their input increased their commitment. Over the years, we learned that, as a leader, when it came to casting a vision, you have to strike a balance between analysis and planning on your own, and input and suggestions from the team.

A key component in our approach to building the team was to give people flexibility in how they went about conducting their work and spending their time. We worked hard to keep the company policy manual as thin as possible, believing that people should use their best judgment about how to handle situations, as opposed to us creating a policy manual to address every situation that team members might encounter. Frankly, we had seen far too many companies trying to create a policy for everything only to realize that people can be much more creative than any policy manual can address.

Our paid time off (PTO) policy reflected this approach. It essentially said, "As long as your project is on schedule and your client it happy with your efforts, feel free to take off time from work." We weren't counting days. We weren't overly concerned about where you worked from or how you scheduled your day. We simply expected employees to take care of their clients and they were free to structure their time however best suited them. As the company started to grow, we received more and more questions about the policy. People wanted more guidance and direction. They wanted to know how many PTO days they would get per year, if days would carry over from one year to the next, and a myriad of other parameters about the program.

Jamie and I decided that the best way to handle the situation was to let them come up with their own plan, and that's what they did. I can tell you letting go of this was not an easy choice on our part. We spent hours talking to each other about it, but in the end, we decided that giving them the freedom to create their own plan was worth the trade-off in going against our desire to avoid bureaucracy.

Over the course of several weeks, they formed a committee, solicited input from everyone in the firm, studied what other companies were doing, and built their program. The committee shared the new PTO policy with the rest of the firm, explaining that they would stick with it for a year and make refinements from there.

Guess what?

Everyone hated it. They became frustrated with the limitations they had placed upon themselves. Within the first few months, it was evident that people wanted to go in a new direction, but to their credit they stuck with their plan for the entire year. Exactly one year from the day they launched the new PTO policy, they scrapped their own plan. I wish I could say that they ran back to the plan Jamie and I created, praising us for the inherent brilliance of our approach, but that would be a lie. What we created wasn't meeting their needs as they collectively craved more guidance and direction. So, they created something new—something based on our unique business. It involved a degree of recognition for seniority, flexibility as needed, and an emphasis on doing what was right for our clients. It was simple, elegant, and effective.

By letting go and letting them create their plan, a better answer was ultimately uncovered. Frankly, the entire process was difficult for Jamie and me. At times, we wanted to jump in and save the day. We wanted to set the new PTO policy on fire in front of the entire team and make an edict that we were going back to the old ways, our ways. Had the PTO policy been causing employee turnover or hurting our client work, I'm sure we would have intervened, but that wasn't the case. The policy was more of a nuisance and a source of frustration for people as they had given away flexibility for something too draconian.

As a leader, your job is not to control everything. Trying to control everything is both unrealistic (remember my parachute story from Day 1) and undesirable. Why is it undesirable? You are surrounded by people who possess amazing talents, unlimited potential, and boundless creativity—the value of which is realized not through control, but release. Your job as a leader is to let go of things in order to release the brilliance of others.

DAY 26: LET GO

Today's Thought

Effective leadership involves letting go of some things as opposed to trying to control everything.

Today's Questions

1. Have you experienced a time when a leader let go of something and allowed the team to take the reins? What happened?

   _____

   _____

2. How have you tried to strike a balance between letting go and controlling? Has this served you well?

   _____

   _____

Today's Challenge

Identify one thing (big or small) that you are holding on to and let go of it by giving it to someone else to handle today.

**DAY
27**

PLAY TO WIN

With fifteen minutes to go until my 8:00 a.m. meeting, I was walking briskly across the parking lot toward the building's front door. Time was tight, but I was confident that I could grab a quick coffee and slip into my seat at the conference table with a couple of minutes to spare.

Then, my phone rang. I looked down, saw the name on my screen, and greeted the caller with, "Good morning, how are you?"

The response on the other end of the line was a frantic, "Help!"

EIGHT WEEKS EARLIER

It was late November and I was in the process of helping one of my clients—let's call her Darlene—and her team as they worked to set their priorities for the upcoming tax season. Darlene and her team members are accountants at a regional accounting firm and they had decided that they wanted to improve in a few key areas. In the United States, the busiest season for most accountants is from the beginning of the calendar year until mid-April. It is during this time that Darlene and her team receive documentation from their clients, prepare taxes, and submit paperwork for their clients to file or extend by the April 15 due date. Late hours and seven-day-a-week schedules are common during this period. It's part of the job.

With about forty days to go before the onslaught of tax season, Darlene and her team members had a robust brainstorming session in which they identified the one priority that they truly felt was most important. With my help, they gained clarity on the priority and crafted a statement that clearly articulated how they performed last tax season and the improvements they wanted to make during the upcoming period.

As they went through the process of identifying their top priority and establishing their plan, I encouraged them to ensure that both the priority and the plan worked together to create a winnable game. I explained that within each of us there seems to be some kind of *game-on* switch. For some the switch is more easily flipped than for others. Regardless of one's willingness to throw the switch, once engaged, it can dramatically increase engagement. The key is often to ensure that our priorities and plans make work a game worth playing. This may sound simple, but it is rare because few organizations have mastered the art of making work winnable, which causes far too many employees to settle for playing not to lose. Playing not to lose often leads to people avoiding risks, watching the clock, and being content with just getting through the day. It's difficult to accomplish anything significant when everyone is just trying to get through the day.

I shared with Darlene and her team that they can benefit from making work more engaging if they ensure that the priorities they set and the plans they create take ten key game-building items into consideration.

TEN GAME-BUILDING KEYS

1. **Identify a worthy but defeatable opponent.** Playing a game is a costly endeavor. It takes time, energy, and resources. If the opponent is easily beaten, people disengage. They also disengage if the opponent is unbeatable. So make sure that every priority you set is worth the effort to win.

2. **Create clear rules by which to play.** If the rules of the game are not appropriate for the undertaking, not clearly defined, and inconsistently applied, players will lose interest—or worse—become cynical. So make sure everyone understands what rules are in place as they work to accomplish their priorities.

3. **Clarify the consequences—winning or losing matters.** People care about a game when the outcome matters. If no consequences for

winning or losing exist, players simply won't care about the game. So make sure that every team member has a way to share in the win when the priority is achieved.

4. **Challenge the players.** The best games challenge players to put themselves to the test—unleashing their best knowledge, skills, talents, and abilities to win the game. So ensure that everyone has a part to play.

5. **Strive for a fast pace—or at least an appropriate pace.** To keep players engaged, the scoreboard needs to change often. When a game moves too slowly, players may become uninterested or move to another game. As a result, the original game is abandoned. So make sure that the plan breaks activities down to a level where employees can show weekly progress.

6. **Ensure the players interact with each other—the play of others impacts what you do.** The best games involve team member interaction. One player's move may support, enhance, or complement another team member's actions or may cause a change to his plan, strategy, or play. So make sure the plan encourages teamwork.

7. **Keep playing to become a better player.** The act of playing the game sharpens a player's ability to play future games and develops essential decisionmaking, problem-solving, and leadership skills. So make sure that the plan not only challenges each team member, but that it allows them to stay in the game until the priority is accomplished.

8. **Reward successful play.** As the game unfolds, players must be recognized for great play—in much the same way athletes get cheers and video gamers get points. Small, timely rewards encourage people to play longer and harder. So make sure the plan allows for frequent small wins on the way to victory on the priority.

9. **Make it a game of choice.** Games of chance can be fun for a while, but less rewarding than games of choice in the long term. Many people disengage when they realize the game of chance requires no skill and may not be winnable. Employees prefer games in which they can predict the outcomes of their actions and which require them to choose how best to play. So make sure that the priorities you set and the plans you create are within reach of your team based upon their efforts and not solely reliant on outside forces.

10. **Reflect and celebrate.** Playing and winning matters, and so players take tremendous pride from their efforts and results. The person who plays and wins a winnable game speaks positively about the experience and often admits that the time, effort, and resources expended were worth the sacrifice. Celebration brings one winning season to a close and prepares the players for the next. So make sure you build into the plan time to celebrate and learn from the victory. Don't just rush off to the next priority.

In the November meeting, Darlene and her team put time and energy into ensuring that both the priority they set for themselves and the plan to accomplish the priority satisfied each of the ten items outlined above. They then built a team scoreboard to track their progress. It felt good and the team ended the meeting on a high.

Now back to the 8:00 a.m. phone call.

I followed Darlene's request for help with a question about what was going on. She told me that they were making no progress on the priority. In fact, performance was lower than the previous year.

I asked, "Well, what does the team think about the fact that they are losing at the game they created for themselves?"

After several seconds, Darlene sheepishly said, "They don't know how they are doing," and went on to explain that she never posted the scoreboard.

My response was, "Please go out into the team's work area, hang up the scoreboard, and call me at 4:00 p.m."

At 4:00 p.m., Darlene and I reconnected. She explained that the team was frustrated because they realized they were losing. She added that the worst part was that they were frustrated with her because she hadn't told them the score and they didn't realize that they were losing.

In the end, the team was able to turn the game around and delivered their best performance ever. In preparing for their next year's tax season, they committed to a higher goal and Darlene committed to having the scoreboard up on day one.

As you transition into today's thought, questions, and challenge, use this as an opportunity to consider how you can help yourself and others to win.

DAY 27: PLAY TO WIN

Today's Thought

Coupling an important priority with an engaging plan is a recipe for turning work into a winnable game.

Today's Questions

1. Have you ever found yourself playing not to lose in a job? What was the situation?

   _____

   _____

2. Have you ever found yourself playing to win in a job? What was the situation?

   _____

   _____

3. How would you describe the difference in your attitude, commitment, and enthusiasm when comparing your answers in these two situations?

   _____

   _____

Today's Challenge

Think of someone that you believe is very engaged in her work. Ask that person how they know if they are winning or losing on things that matter.

HIT PAUSE AND ENGAGE

I was sitting across the table from a truly successful salesperson. In fact, he was so successful that he was promoted from regional sales manager in one business unit to global innovation leader for the entire company. Although he had far less experience than his predecessor, his knowledge of the business, personal drive, and track record for delivering results suggested that he was fully up for the challenge. The new innovation leader had asked me to meet with him to discuss his priorities for the year and the plan that his team was going to execute. In all honesty, I was impressed. The priorities appeared sound and well aligned to the organization's strategy, and the plan he laid out made sense.

When I asked him how involved his people were in helping to set the priorities and develop the plan, it was as if a switch was thrown. He went from speaking in detail about the plan to generalities in regard to his team members' involvement. He said things like, "We talked about it the other day in a meeting," or "They are pretty familiar with where things are going." It became clear to me that he was speaking in code as the truth was likely closer to something like, "I actually did most of the prioritizing and planning on my own."

It was apparent that he knew where my line of questioning was headed, because he jumped out in front of my next couple of questions by explaining that he was confident in the priorities and plans. Yes, he may have acted a bit more on his own than he would've liked, but he was under a time crunch and getting everyone involved would've taken a lot of time. Nonetheless, he felt good about the incentives that he created and how the team would execute the plan.

Fearful that he might get a bit defensive and not wanting to offend, I simply said, "In all honesty, I'm impressed with what you have shared with me. You have clearly invested tremendous time, energy, and brainpower to create this. You should be very proud of the work that you have done." Pausing for a moment to let my comments land, I then added, "I just have two concerns. First, your background is in sales, but your new team is made up primarily of engineers and designers. Is it possible that what you consider to be an incentive is different than what your people may find motivating? Second, your plan seems very solid to me, but I'm an outsider and my understanding of your work is limited. I can only imagine the time pressure that you are under to deliver results, but might it make sense to get a few of your people, the ones who touch the work every day, to take a look at everything?"

Thankfully, he agreed and within a few short hours he was able to get several of his team members to review everything with him. As I thought might be the case, they had some suggestions for him to consider and they were thankful that he had asked. Of equal importance, he was grateful that they helped him to think through a couple of issues that he hadn't considered.

As a leader, you will never have enough time and you will often feel the pressure to move fast. However, your desire for speed may come at a cost. Sometimes, you have to hit pause and engage your team. In all likelihood, you understand this at an intellectual level, but you may have a tremendous obstacle to overcome in order to act on this information. You're busy. Your day is consumed with meetings, phone calls, emails, and a vast number of time-stealing activities. You spend your workday running from issue to issue with barely any time to think. This is a recipe for employee engagement problems.

Allow me to provide four specific opportunities when you should hit pause and engage people.

1. SHARE EXPECTATIONS AND DON'T ASSUME CLARITY

Imagine this. You catch an employee in the hallway and ask him to take care of something. He doesn't quite know what to do, but attempts to tackle the work.

You think you empowered him; he feels abandoned. In the end, you are frustrated with the results. He is frustrated with your reaction and begins to disengage.

Next time, hit pause and try this:

Instead of assigning the task in the hallway, schedule a time to sit down with the employee. Discuss what needs to be done, why it matters, and share your expectations for the effort. Allow him to ask clarifying questions. Then, together, get clear on the resources needed and how the two of you will work together to discuss progress.

2. REMOVE OBSTACLES AND DON'T OWN AN EMPLOYEE'S PROBLEMS

One of your employees is working on an important project. She is struggling with a portion of the work. She catches you at the end of the day and explains the problem. You realize you can easily take care of it yourself. So, you offer to fix the issue and take it from her. You feel helpful. She's relieved. Unfortunately, she misses a chance to work her way through an issue and learn something new. Unwittingly, she takes a step closer to disengagement.

Next time, hit pause and try this:

Sit down and discuss the issue. Work with her to brainstorm options, offer suggestions, and then allow her to select a path. Be willing to use your position to help her succeed, but don't own the problem for her. If you take it, she won't learn how to deal with the issue next time, and there's always a next time.

3. UNDERSTAND MOTIVATIONS AND DON'T FORCE-FIT INCENTIVES

In order to achieve a goal, you decide to implement an incentive program. Money motivates you, so you figure it will motivate your people, too. You send out an email announcing your great incentive. Some team members latch on to the idea (money motivates them, as well) and they begin to do what you hoped they would. Others, who have different motivations, don't get as excited about the incentive. They work harder because they know you are wanting a different result, but they don't push themselves as you'd hoped. The incentive period ends and you give bonuses to the winners. The folks motivated by money are more engaged than ever. The ones who didn't win start working on their resumes.

Next time, hit pause and try this:

Bring your employees together. Explain the goal you hope to achieve and ask each of them what they would consider a reward if the team accomplished the goal. You might learn that a few people want more money, but some may appreciate time off or an opportunity to attend a conference or training program. Then, design an incentive program that is fair to all, yet tailored to the motivations of the individual.

4. GIVE YOUR ATTENTION AND DON'T MULTITASK THE CONVERSATION

I have a friend who says, "When a leader is multitasking, it means that someone is getting ignored." She has a point.

Perhaps you have experienced times when an employee stops by your office. The timing isn't good for you, but you allow the conversation to start. You are less than fully engaged. You are reading email, thinking about an upcoming meeting, and "listening" to your direct report. In all likelihood, the email can wait, the meeting will come in good time, but the employee may choose to disengage you and the organization.

Next time, hit pause and try this:

If an employee swings by your office with a request to talk, give her your undivided attention and turn off the distractions. If you truly have a pressing issue that can't wait, let her know that you want to talk, but the timing isn't right. Explain the conflict and commit to a specific time to connect in the near future.

Then, guard that time and uphold your commitment.

DAY 28: HIT PAUSE AND ENGAGE

Today's Thought

Sometimes the best thing a leader can do in the moment is to hit pause and engage the team.

Today's Questions

1. In addition to time pressures, there are many other reasons that a leader might not hit pause and engage. What do you think are some barriers to hitting pause and engaging others?

2. Who do you work with that might benefit from you choosing to hit pause and engaging with them? How and when could you start to better meet this person's needs?

Today's Challenge

Explain today's lesson to a friend, colleague, or family member. Ask that person to share a time when choosing to hit pause and engaging someone else made a big difference. Follow up with a question about how he felt in the moment.

WEEK 4 WRAP-UP

Throughout Week 4, you have learned several planning considerations. The concepts of ownership, imagination, relationships, openness, engagement, and everything else that you explored this week are key to effectively leading yourself and others to create plans. Now it is time for you to put this week's lessons to work as you plan how you will accomplish your priorities.

In this section, you will put two simple planning formats into practice depending on the type of priorities that you set for yourself. One format is designed for project priorities and the other is for process priorities. Think of it this way. If you were to set one priority to build a home gym and a second priority to lose weight, creating the gym is a project priority. It has a specific start and stop date and is designed to create something once. You will accomplish each task in the plan and then move on to the next task until the home gym is up and running. On the other hand, losing weight is a process goal. You will pick weight loss behaviors and continue to repeat and refine those behaviors as you work to win on your priority. You won't go for one run or lift a few weights and claim victory. Like it or not, you will likely finish many workouts on your way to accomplishing your goal.

Whether you are creating a plan on your own for a personal priority or working with a team to achieve results together, the two formats will serve you well.

Here are the steps to follow:

1. Pick one of your Week 3 priorities.

_____

2. Determine if the selected priority is a project or a process priority.

_____

_____

3. For project priorities, complete the Project Priority Planning form by answering:

    a. Who?_____

    b. Does what?_____

    c. By when?_____

4. For process priorities, complete the Process Priority Planning form by answering:

    a. Who?_____

    b. Does what?_____

    c. To what standard?_____

    d. How often?_____

Project Priority Plan

Priority: _____

_____

_____

_____

Who?	Does What?	By When?

Process Priority Plan

Priority: _____

_____

_____

_____

Who?	Does What?	By What Standard?	How Often?

WEEK 5

INSPIRE PERFORMANCE

When I was in the military, we had a very consistent regimen. Every morning of the week, we would get up early and go for a run. We would run three, four, five, or more miles every day. We did it whether it was raining or the sun was shining. It was a habit for us, and over time, most of us, became pretty good at it.

One day, a friend asked me if I would be interested in running a marathon with him. Having never run 26.2 miles (42 kilometers) in my life, I said what any young person full of energy would say: "Absolutely, let's do it!" Over the course of the next several weeks, we trained for the marathon. Truth be told, we never went over twenty miles (thirty-two kilometers) in a single run, but we did log a few runs in the teens.

When the weekend of the big race came, we hit the road after work on Friday, drove to the race site, stayed in a hotel a few miles from the starting line, and headed out early the next morning to begin our marathon. The race went well. We finished slightly faster than the goal we had set for ourselves, were able to enjoy our time on the run, took a quick shower after the race, and drove back home. That Monday, we did our normal workout routine. Yes, our legs were a bit tired, but we were fine.

The habit of running daily + youth = a strong performance.

Fast-forward several years. I was no longer in the military, but I set a priority for myself to run another marathon. I made the decision right after I hit one of those birthdays that end in a five or a zero. Those milestones can often drive us to set new priorities. After talking with Jamie and the kids, I signed myself up for the Walt Disney World Marathon. I convinced myself that tackling 26.2 miles at the Happiest Place on Earth made perfect sense. The race was in January, so the weather would be relatively mild, and Disney World is pretty flat so there wouldn't be many hills to slow me down.

I then went to my computer and created the perfect plan for running a marathon. My plan allowed me to go from my current fitness level to one that would be comparable to, if not surpass, what I had achieved when I was in the army. The plan called for a gradual weekly ramp-up of mileage, followed by a tapering off just prior to the event. I saw myself standing at the starting line more ready than ever before. The plan was beautiful, at least on paper.

Unfortunately, life got in the way and my grand plan started to unravel. Little things caused me to lose sight of the plan.

- On a couple of occasions, my colleagues needed help with something first thing in the morning, so I skipped my morning workout to get them what they needed. I promised myself that I would run later in the day, but that didn't happen.
- There was the time when one of our kids became sick in the middle of the night and Jamie and I spent the wee hours of the morning attending to the illness. I said that I would make up for the missed mileage later in the week; however, the next few mornings I hit the snooze button with my hand, instead of the pavement with my feet.
- A number of times, business trips got in the way of my daily exercise plans. Leaving town early in the morning and flying back later that night left no time to work out.

The list goes on and on, but you get the point. My plans were suffering at the hands of many viable excuses, but they were suffering nonetheless.

Eventually, race day arrived. Despite not preparing as I had planned, I still found myself standing at the starting line at 5:00 a.m. outside of one of Walt Disney World's theme parks. If you know Disney World, you know that Disney does nothing small. Even in the early hours of the day, they brought the excitement. Mickey stood on scaffolding high above the starting line, music was blaring, the countdown started, and fireworks were launched to mark the beginning of the race. Off we went.

If you've ever participated in a large run, you likely know that unless you are toward the front of the group, you aren't doing a lot of running at first. That day, I was about two-thirds of the way back in the pack of seven thousand runners. So I pretty much walked and jogged for the first mile. I was feeling good. As I approached mile-marker number one, I heard music playing and caught a glimpse of a familiar Disney character awaiting our arrival. I high-fived the character to mark the first of the twenty-six miles (forty-one kilometers) and continued on to mile number two where I greeted two Disney characters with a high five for each. I was feeling pretty darn good.

At about mile ten, my inability to execute my preparation plan caught up with me. I started to realize that it didn't matter how much music they pumped through the speakers or who they shoved in a costume; I was running out of gas. The next sixteen miles were a grind. I was out of high fives, my legs hurt, my feet were sore, and I was ready to call it a day. Around mile eighteen, I caught the eye of a supporter who was standing along the race route. She had a child on her hip, an infant in a stroller, and a toddler standing adjacent to her. By all accounts, she had a lot going on, but in that moment, she saw my pain. In an effort to encourage me, she shouted out, "Push yourself, you can do it!" I appreciated the sentiment, but in my mind I was thinking, "No, I can't. I had a great plan but failed to implement it. Now, my performance is in the tank."

If you are wondering, yes, I finished the race, but it wasn't pretty. I completed it at a much slower pace than I had run in the past and recovered much more slowly. However, I learned an important lesson about the relationship between planning and performance. Although the planning process is critical and plans themselves are important, it is through consistent execution of those plans that results are achieved and people reach their full potential.

This week, you are going to explore what it takes to perform on your priorities both on your own and with team members. You will explore various lessons about how to approach performance and what you can learn from others who have struggled and succeeded on their own journeys. By the end of the week, you will draft your Leadership Legacy Statement indicating what you want to achieve as a leader, how you will work with and through others to accomplish results, and how you want to be remembered as a leader.

DAY 29

UNDERSTAND INCONSISTENCY

O ver the years, I have had the pleasure of working with some amazing people. These included brave paratroopers in the army, talented professionals for our company, and brilliant students at Vanderbilt University. I've been inspired by those whom I worked with in each situation.

I've also been frustrated by soldiers who weren't doing what I repeatedly asked them to do, employees who needed to be reminded over and over again about how to properly submit expense reports, and college pupils who wait until the very last moment to work on an assignment despite it being spelled out in the syllabus and talked about since the very beginning of the semester.

The most quizzical thing about the soldiers, employees, and students listed above is that those whom I would list as examples in the amazing group are the same people I would list as examples in the frustrating group.

The reality is that people (you and me included) are often inconsistent in our behavior. This can be very frustrating, especially as a leader. There will be instances when you feel like you have talked about something ad nauseam and explained everything in excruciating detail, yet your employees will do the right thing one time and the wrong thing the next time. In some organizations, inconsistent performance to established standards is an epidemic.

Even more difficult is employees embracing new behaviors to drive better results. Let's face it. It's hard enough to change your own behavior, but changing the behavior of someone else, or an entire team of people, can seem impossible.

If you find that your people aren't doing what you want them to do, they are falling prey to what I call the ABCs of employee behavior. I'm not trying to be overly simplistic here, but if you consider the reason(s) someone isn't doing something, the answer will typically fall into one or more of these areas:

ATTITUDE:
PEOPLE AREN'T MOTIVATED TO DO IT

Getting a paycheck alone isn't motivation enough, especially in a world of expanding choices. Your people need to want it as much as you want it.

Consider these questions:

- Why does this matter to my people?
- What is the bigger win for them if we make this happen?
- Do I have their backs and hands only, or their minds and hearts, too?

BIG PICTURE:
PEOPLE DON'T KNOW WHAT NEEDS TO BE DONE

Your people need to understand what exactly it is you are trying to achieve. They need to understand how their effort fits into a bigger goal.

Consider these questions:

- How exactly are we going to measure success?
- If we accomplish this at my level, how does it impact the organization?

CAPABILITIES:
PEOPLE DON'T HAVE THE SKILLS TO MAKE IT HAPPEN

Being motivated to do something is important, as is understanding what the team is trying to accomplish. At some point, however, people need to be able to deliver the goods. They need to know how to do whatever it is that they need to accomplish.

Consider these questions:

- What does each person need to do to ensure success?
- How do we make sure we are properly trained to do the work?
- What gaps exist within our team that we need to close?

Systems:
PEOPLE AREN'T ALWAYS OPERATING IN A SYSTEM
THAT CONSISTENTLY SUPPORTS THE RIGHT BEHAVIORS

While the first three are the responsibility of both leaders and team members, this one falls squarely on the shoulders of the leader. Employees work within systems, but leaders work on systems.

Consider these questions:

- Do the systems you and your organization have in place help people deliver results?
- Are your systems causing people to jump through unnecessary hoops, creating frivolous roadblocks, or zapping the very energy out of each and every one of your team members?

A key part of understanding the ABCs is recognizing that, as a leader, you play a huge role in getting them right.

- **Attitude.** You can do a lot to inspire your people when they are struggling with motivation issues.
- **Big Picture.** You can work to more effectively communicate to your people why the organization is going in a particular direction or explain the thinking behind a policy or program.
- **Capabilities.** You can assist your people in developing the skills they need today and in the future if they are struggling with capabilities.
- **Systems.** You can create systems that elevate your performance, rather than dragging people down.

DAY 29: UNDERSTAND INCONSISTENCY

Today's Thought

We appear to be wired for consistent inconsistency. Fortunately, you hold the power to help yourself and others to overcome inconsistency by understanding the importance of attitude, big picture, capabilities, and systems.

Today's Questions

1. Think of a behavior in which your performance is inconsistent. If you had to identify which of the ABCs is contributing to your inconsistency, which one(s) would you pick and why?

   _____

   _____

2. How might you address the underlying issues that are causing your inconsistency?

   _____

   _____

Today's Challenge

Take action today on addressing the underlying issue you identified in your answer to the above question. A small step today can make a big difference in the long run.

DAY 30

PRACTICE ABUNDANCE

On the second floor of a fairly nondescript office building, I was interviewed to join KPMG Consulting. Up until that point, I had spent the majority of my adult life in the army, so the job was intriguing on many fronts. The prospect of wearing a business suit every day and helping clients to solve problems was interesting, so when a friend suggested that I apply for a position, I spruced up my resume and filled out the application. I sat for an in-person interview shortly thereafter. Getting a tour of the office, meeting my potential colleagues, and learning a bit about the role sealed the deal. So, when they called to offer me the position, I happily accepted.

What I didn't understand at the time was that joining the firm as junior consultant was a bit like playing a game in Vegas. You roll the dice and depending on which boss you get and which client engagement you are assigned to, your initial experience in the company could be far different from the person hired just before you or the one hired right after you. In my case, the dice returned a somewhat mixed outcome. On one hand, my engagement proved to be life-changing. I ended up with a client, let's call him Peter, who was very abundant. Peter valued me, supported my efforts, challenged me, and actively looked for ways to help me and my colleagues win. Peter took my team into his confidence and promoted our efforts with his boss and others in his organization. I have had a lot of great clients over the years, but Peter was top of the top.

The other die I cast didn't end up quite as well. The KPMG partner, let's call him Harry, I was assigned to proved to be far less abundant than my client, Peter. Where Peter was helpful, Harry relied on intimidation and fear. Prone to moments of anger, Harry would openly embarrass my colleagues when their projects stumbled. He doled out harsh criticism for all to hear. Fortunately for me, my client work was going very well. The project was expanding, my team was growing, and Peter paid his bills on time. That turned out to be a recipe for success and Harry pretty much left me to my own devices. My interactions with Harry were limited and, due to the demands of my project work, I spent most of my time on the client's site.

Over time, I learned of another KPMG partner, let's call him Greg, who operated in a different part of the same nondescript second floor. Those who landed on this partner's team benefited from a similar fate as those who worked for my client. Greg was also very abundant. He openly praised people who performed well and offered private feedback and coaching when they struggled. His team members enjoyed working for him because they felt supported and encouraged.

I've spent considerable time thinking about these leaders as they had a profound impact on how I chose to lead others later in my career. Because of them, I have invested much effort to study the concepts of scarcity and abundance. My efforts thus far have yielded eight behaviors of truly abundant leaders.

Collectively, these behaviors are not only the indication of a truly abundant leader, they are more often than not the sign of a genuinely happy and effective one. If you want to achieve sustained and exceptional performance, you should work to embrace these eight abundant leadership behaviors.

1. GIVE OTHERS CREDIT

Abundant leaders care little about getting credit for themselves. They believe that great ideas can come from any source and there's no limit on sources or ideas, so they aren't compelled to steal someone else's limelight. In fact, they believe that shining the light on those who contribute makes everyone a bit brighter.

2. ASK FOR INPUT

Not seeing themselves as the only source of good ideas or fearing the scrutiny that might come from asking others for help and support, abundant leaders willingly and actively solicit the input of others. They do this, not because they want to create a fake sense of involvement or buy-in, but because they believe that the active participation of many creates a better solution.

3. EXTEND TRUST

Abundant leaders pour out trust upon others. This doesn't mean that they are gullible or refuse to recognize the risks of failure; it simply means they know that in order to achieve the best results today and tomorrow, they must trust others and create a trusting culture. They also know that a culture of trust starts with them.

4. COACH OTHERS

Scarce leaders don't take the time to help others. They are too focused on their own career path to care about the journey of another. Abundant leaders not only take the time, but they consider coaching both a duty and a privilege. Helping others become the master is the ultimate reward for an abundant leader.

5. SHARE IDEAS

Because abundant leaders don't care who gets the credit, they are willing to share their ideas. Unlike individuals who wait to spring their brilliant answer on others at just the right time or those who hold back during brainstorming exercises for fear of sounding foolish, abundant leaders are willing to put their ideas on the table and allow the team to build on, improve, or toss the ideas out as appropriate.

6. CONNECT PEOPLE

When someone is seeking a door to be opened or a problem to be solved, abundant leaders are willing to make connections among members of their network. It can be a tough balance between respecting the value of a connection and openly sharing that connection with others, but truly abundant leaders have mastered that challenge. They have a bias to connect and share.

7. MEET UNSPOKEN NEEDS

Abundant leaders are clued into the needs of others and not just themselves, making them more aware of the unspoken needs of those around them. They recognize when someone is struggling with a task, an emotion, or any other challenge and reach out to them with a word of encouragement and an offer to help.

8. LISTEN MORE

The truly abundant leader practices effective listening. They don't merely listen to pick up on the key issues as they formulate a response; they listen to understand. They ask clarifying questions. They try to understand the speaker's perspective. Pretend listening isn't part of the abundant leader's actions.

DAY 30: PRACTICE ABUNDANCE

Today's Thought

Great leaders recognize that being abundant is truly more effective than being scarce.

Today's Questions

1. Have you ever worked for a scarce leader? If so, how did it feel working for someone who practiced scarce behaviors?

    _____

    _____

2. Have you ever worked for an abundant leader? If so, how did it feel working for someone who was truly abundant?

    _____

    _____

3. Would people describe you as more abundant or scarce? Why?

    _____

    _____

Today's Challenge

Think of an abundant leader that you know and ask her this question: "I've noticed that you choose to be abundant in how you lead others. How has that approach served you and your teams well over the years?"

DAY 31

FORGO (SOME) HAPPINESS

My team and I had been working with a large client to implement a number of talent-management programs across an eight-thousand-person organization. Each program was designed to better attract, develop, position, and retain talent. My team's efforts led to the creation of an organization-wide coaching initiative, the establishment of several leadership development courses, a partnership with an academic institution for a tailored graduate studies degree, and a certification program to ensure that employees had the necessary education, training, and experience.

Designing, developing, implementing, and evaluating programs like these are complex endeavors. There are many moving pieces, all of which require a great deal of coordination and communication. As we received approval for the programs and set out to implement them, our efforts shifted from the organization's executive corridors where big priorities are approved to the front line where performance actually occurs.

I'll never forget the day I met Diane, a human resources analyst on the organization's talent team. We quickly hit it off and became fast friends. She was upbeat, welcoming, and excited about the coaching program. Well, she was excited about it until she learned that the new program was going to cause her to change some of the things that she had been doing. Diane was going to have to change a few of the spreadsheets and forms that she used in her job. She would have to go to a few meetings as the program unfolded and then a weekly status meeting once the coaching program was fully implemented. Plus, Diane was going to need to learn a new software tool that was being used to administer the program. She didn't like any of it. Suddenly, my newfound friend wanted me to go away and never return to her workspace. She was not excited about how the big strategy was going to change things in her corner of the world.

When Diane told her boss about the changes and her reluctance to embrace them, he listened to her concerns and showed empathy for Diane's situation. He then told her that, although he understood and valued her perspective, the decision had been made and everyone was going to have to change things in order to make the program work. Diane left the meeting disappointed in his decision, but she felt heard and understood. She was still a bit miffed with me.

Change is an inevitable part of our world. The status quo rarely stays the status quo. Effective leaders understand this reality and they further understand that not everyone is happy with the prospect of change. If you have ever led a team through a change, you have likely experienced pushback from your people as they struggle with feelings of discomfort, a loss of power, fear of failure, and a desire to return to their perception of normal. Effective leaders also know that change can lead to growth, pride, success, and a new and improved normal. So they embrace an important paradox:

In order to avoid disappointing your team members, you must, at times, disappoint them.

This statement may appear absurd and self-contradictory—that's the nature of a paradox. However, wise leaders know that it is based on sound reasoning.

This doesn't mean that wise leaders go out of their way to disappoint employees. That's cruel, shortsighted, and truly unwise. It simply means that wise leaders are willing to forgo short-term employee happiness for long-term employee growth, development, and fulfillment.

Let's face it. Immature, inexperienced, and unsure leaders often violate this paradox.

I know that I have violated it myself in an effort to avoid conflict, please an employee, expedite a solution, control a situation, or some other seemingly well-intended reason. Each violation came at the cost of our collective ability to perform at the highest level.

I offer four examples of situations where leaders tend to get this wrong, and I recommend that you consider each of these as you work to execute your priorities.

1. THE LEADER FAILS TO GIVE CANDID AND TIMELY FEEDBACK

Sitting across the desk from someone and giving critical feedback can be difficult. Some leaders are people-pleasers. They tend to sugarcoat the bad and accentuate the positive. True, the leader could be more direct, but that might make things a bit uncomfortable. So, he opts to say something like, "Things didn't go as well as I'd hoped, but let's try harder next year."

The employee is pleased that the performance review is over and she emerges unscathed. The leader appears understanding and compassionate.

What's the harm?

2. THE LEADER TAKES A TEAM MEMBER'S PROBLEM

It is not uncommon for an employee to run into a problem as she goes about her work. When faced with an employee struggling, many leaders want to jump in and solve the employee's problem. After all, who doesn't want to be the superhero swooping in to save the day?

The employee is satisfied that the problem is solved. The leader appears competent and helpful.

What's the harm?

3. THE LEADER ACCOMPLISHES A TEAM MEMBER'S WORK

Consider an employee who is new to his role. He's frustrated that he is struggling with one of his new tasks. Along comes the seasoned leader who can tackle the task in a few minutes. She simply makes a couple of phone calls and writes a quick email—presto! All is accomplished.

The employee is satisfied that the task is done. The leader appears capable and impactful.

What's the harm?

4. THE LEADER TELLS
A TEAM MEMBER HOW TO DO SOMETHING

A leader asks an employee to complete a project. After the leader shares the purpose of the initiative, he also explains in detail how the employee should do the work. He provides the tasks, the specific timing, and even how to manage various challenges that might arise.

The employee is satisfied that the planning task is done. The leader appears powerful and confident.

What's the harm?

Here's the harm. Each of the four above situations involves short-term thinking on behalf of the leader, which eliminates the opportunity for an employee to learn, grow, and develop. In the long run, the employee will be dissatisfied because she will be less competitive, less competent, and less prepared for future challenges.

DAY 31: FORGO (SOME) HAPPINESS

Today's Thought

In order to avoid disappointing your team members, you must, at times, disappoint them.

Today's Questions

1. Have there been times in the past where you chose short-term employee satisfaction to the detriment of long-term satisfaction?

   _____

   _____

   _____

2. If so, what caused you to make these choices (e.g., desire to appease, fear of looking unhelpful, lack of patience, etc.)?

   _____

   _____

   _____

3. Which team members would benefit from being pushed and stretched?

   _____

   _____

   _____

4. What tasks could you give them that would cause a bit of disappointment
    now, but tremendous growth in the future?

    _____

    _____

    _____

Today's Challenge

Consider a change that you went through in recent years that you were reluctant
to embrace. With the perspective of time, write down how working your way
through that change caused you to learn, grow, and develop.

DAY 32

ADDRESS ELEPHANTS

The team was wrapped around the conference table in our Washington, D.C., office engrossed in the conversation. The voices of our fellow teammates from our other office locations emitted from the speakerphone in the center of the table. We were having a company-wide call to discuss the previous quarter's performance and our collective plans for the upcoming period. I enjoyed these conversations because they were a chance to celebrate our accomplishments and collaborate about how to address future opportunities.

One of our D.C. team members, Ben, whom I would've expected to see sitting at the table, had joined us on the phone. In all honesty, I thought nothing of it, assuming that he must have had an early morning meeting, a personal commitment, or something else that required him to be away from the office that morning. When the call finished, I walked down the hallway to my workspace. Along the way, I passed Ben's office. His door was ajar and the lights were on, so I knocked and he invited me in. We exchanged a few pleasantries and I said something to the fact that he must have just arrived at the office since he had joined the call remotely.

Ben's answer stunned me. "Nope," he said. "I find it easier to take those calls from my office. I'm not big on all of the collaboration we do around here."

Collaboration was something we valued at our firm and had been key to our success. How could he have possibly joined the conference call from down the hall?

Yellow flags were everywhere, but I was pressed for time. So, I said something benign like, "Next time, please come down to the conference room and join the team. You were missed."

About a week later, another team member informed me of problems that she was having with Ben. He had missed a couple of deadlines and, in her words, "blew off" her requests for a status update on his project work. We both agreed that Ben's actions were out of line. We discussed how she might approach Ben in the future and she agreed to give it a try. A week later, I asked her how the conversation went with Ben. She explained that she hadn't had a chance to talk to him yet because of customer obligations, but would do it soon. Her reasoning for not having the conversation was justified at one level. She did have several pressing things on her plate that demanded her attention. Much like the meeting I was rushing to earlier when I encountered Ben in his office, these other issues needed to be attended to, but so did Ben's behavior.

You are no doubt familiar with the expression "Don't ignore the elephant in the room." The saying refers to an issue that no one in the organization talks about, but everyone knows exists.

Some elephants are thrust upon an organization by external forces (e.g., the economy, regulatory issues, etc.). However, many elephants are the direct result of allowing baby elephants to mature in plain sight. Here are a few examples of the latter:

- A project that is doomed, but so much energy and political cache has been invested in the effort that no one is willing to scrap it—so good money is thrown after bad.
- An unhealthy or unprofitable customer relationship that was so difficult to acquire in the first place makes termination of the relationship unspeakable.
- A manager who treats everyone poorly but delivers results—the manager needs to go before a lawsuit arrives; however, we choose to ignore the bad behavior in hopes that it will stop on its own.

Left on their own to graze and grow, a baby elephant may eventually squash your ability to perform on your priorities because it will suddenly demand all of your time, energy, and attention. Here are four things for you to consider about the baby elephants in your midst:

1. LITTLE THINGS BECOME BIG THINGS

If you are on a short hike with a broken compass, being off by a degree or two won't matter much. However, if you are walking a long distance, one or two degrees can cause you to end up a long way from your intended destination. Small things matter—especially over time. It's important to understand this and take action before your journey is thrown way off course.

2. YOU'RE NOT TOO BUSY; IT'S YOUR JOB

Many leaders spend their days rushing from meeting to meeting or digging through a virtual email pile. These activities may be important, and certainly keep one busy, but they also cause distraction from more critical issues. Consider the restaurant manager who walks past trash on the floor because he has paperwork to attend to, or the production supervisor who sees a minor safety issue but says nothing because she is racing to a meeting. They may rationalize their lack of action or be so preoccupied that they failed to notice the problems—either way, they are feeding baby elephants.

3. KNOW WHAT RIGHT LOOKS LIKE

A leader can't address a baby elephant if he or she doesn't know what right looks like. Leaders must invest time in learning standard procedures. They need to understand how jobs should be done or how something works. Stepping out of our comfort zone might be required, but we learn nothing when we are comfortable.

4. LEARN HOW TO GIVE FEEDBACK

Another reason that people ignore baby elephants is because they aren't comfortable giving feedback to employees, much less peers or supervisors. An organization will spend substantial money installing a performance management system, yet fail to invest time teaching people how to give open, candid feedback. Sure, a talent management system is important, but it doesn't outweigh the ability to directly address issues.

DAY 32: ADDRESS ELEPHANTS

Today's Thought

Little things often become big things. Make sure that you feed and care for the little things that you want to see grow and address those that you want to stop in their tracks.

Today's Questions

1. What baby elephants have you experienced in the past that no one addressed? What happened when the elephant grew up?

    _____

    _____

2. Are you caring and feeding for a baby elephant right now? What's the impact over time if you don't address it?

    _____

    _____

Today's Challenge

Regarding your answer to the last question about a baby elephant that is currently in your midst, determine one step that you could take today to begin to address it. Take that step today.

UNLEASH EXCITEMENT

I strongly believe that each of us possesses more energy, creativity, and potential than we bring to our daily roles. This is likely true for your team members and for you. I also contend that if you can learn to tap into what motivates yourself and others, you can unleash tremendous excitement—the type of excitement needed to help you tackle even bigger challenges.

When Clay was a high school senior, he asked if I would take him on a weekend hike with a friend or two. I agreed. Then, things started to change.

Inspired by Bill Bryson's *A Walk in the Woods*, Clay's plan and his excitement grew and grew. What was originally pitched as a weekend camping excursion with two friends turned into ten days of hiking the Appalachian Trail with seven high school seniors. What was initially envisioned as a couple of ten-mile (sixteen-kilometer) days became a hundred miles (161 kilometers) traversing the hills of Georgia and North Carolina. In the end, what I thought would be a "nice thing to do" turned into a great lesson about friendship and what truly matters most. It also taught me an important lesson about what you can learn when you set a priority, perform together, and unleash excitement. When the trip was over, I captured four leadership thoughts that continue to serve me well.

1. JUMP IN

Over the years, I've grown accustomed to sitting on the sidelines watching my kids play or lounging by the side of the pool while they swim. Look around: that's the default role for most adults. Parents watch and kids do.

Hiking the mountains is not a spectator sport. You have to get involved. You must jump in. The same can be true for leaders who fall into the trap of becoming less connected to doing what the frontline employees do. They stop getting their hands dirty, they stop modeling the right behaviors, and their excitement diminishes. Jumping in can create a jolt of excitement for all of us.

2. GET LOST

The Appalachian Trail is marked with 2" x 6" white blazes. If you see the blaze, you are walking on the right path. If you walk for a while and don't see a blaze, you may be lost. Admittedly, there were times when I didn't see a marking for a while and thought we might have veered from the path. When this happened, I became more aware of my surroundings, my eyes darted from side to side, and my heart rate increased. Inevitably, a marked tree would appear around the next bend and all was okay.

Eventually, I figured out that it was difficult to wander from the path and everything would be fine. I began to relax. When, after traveling for a bit, I failed to see a marking, I would simply continue to enjoy the walk and be comfortably lost in the moment. There is a degree of excitement that comes from getting lost in the moment. Great leaders understand this and allow their team to get lost in the work, the customer's world, and dreaming of something bigger together.

3. DEEPEN RELATIONSHIPS

When the hike started, my son and his six friends had known each other for years. They shared the ups and downs of life, held countless sleepovers, mourned the loss of a friend, and were working together to graduate from high school. Before they left, their relationships ran deep. By the end of the trip, their relationships were much deeper. Why? They shared the experience of planning for, conducting, and completing a difficult task. They have memories now that will last a lifetime.

Never underestimate the ability to create and sustain excitement when you allow your people to plan, conduct, and complete a difficult task.

4. CHALLENGE PEOPLE

If you walk long enough, things start to get tough. The boys had their share of challenges. While one dealt with blisters, another had a terribly upset stomach. A couple of the boys slept in a tent that failed to stop the rain one night, and another woke in the morning with serious back pain. Despite the struggles, they all rose to the challenge. Every boy made it up and down every mountain. Every boy carried his own weight. Every one of them is better for meeting the challenge.

Winning is great. Winning begets winning. However, the best and most exciting type of winning comes when you overcome a challenge and win with others. You and your teammates may have no interest in hiking the Appalachian Trail. In fact, you and your teammates may have very different ideas about what interests you, but everyone has something that excites them. Even the most cynical person in your organization is into something. Don't believe me? Take a walk through the parking lot and look at the bumper stickers on their cars, look at the ball caps they wear, ask them what they did this past weekend. You will quickly learn what excites them. Figure out a way to bring some of that to work.

Today's lesson is all about unleashing excitement, the excitement that is in all of us to accomplish things that really matter to us. Sometimes that excitement is dormant. Sometimes people have lost touch with it because of day-to-day activities that have become mundane over time. As you read this lesson, you may be wondering how to actually tap into the excitement of your colleagues.

I encourage you to think about it differently. Every person on your team and everyone in your organization possesses a tremendous amount of excitement just waiting to burst forth. If you don't believe me, consider this. People, your people, get excited about all sorts of things. Some get excited about sporting events, others love opera, and many can't wait for their favorite television show to release the new season. We all get excited about things, even those people who you sometimes feel have no energy or enthusiasm. Your job as a leader is to look for ways to energize yourself and others so that all of you can release your collective excitement in order to accomplish the priorities that truly matter most.

DAY 33: UNLEASH EXCITEMENT

Today's Thought

Every person on your team has something that excites him. It may be buried deep and it may be something that is far removed from work, but it's there. Look for ways to unleash that excitement.

Today's Questions

1. What truly excites you? Is it sports, time with friends, the opera, eighties trivia, or something else?

   _____

   _____

2. How do you feel when you get to do that thing?

   _____

   _____

3. In what ways could the essence of what excites you be brought more into your work?

   _____

   _____

Today's Challenge

Have a conversation with a friend or colleague. Ask her about something that truly excites her. Listen to the words she says and the energy that bubbles to the surface. Consider what that tells you about the excitement in all of us.

FEED CRAVINGS

We were on a roll. What had started as a small training project in which we were hired to create and deliver a mentorship program began to grow quickly and took off nearly overnight. Within a year, it went from being a bit of a side hustle for the firm to our main stage, biggest client, and the team supporting the effort grew from one to several employees. At the eighteen-month point, the project was producing 25 percent of the company's overall revenue, and an ever-expanding team of people was working on the effort. Our client sponsor was thrilled with what we were doing, and we were thrilled, too.

The engagement touched on a range of projects from designing, developing, and delivering multiple training programs at sites around the country, to creating and implementing an employee development plan impacting the careers of thousands of people, to managing internal strategic communications associated with nearly every aspect of the organization's talent-management efforts. Then, our work jumped functions, moving from solely human capital projects to financial management solutions, too. Jamie and I were convinced that we had tapped into something magical.

In most industries, a key success measure is how well you help your customers win on their goals. By that measure, we were killing it. Our client sponsor quickly became a rising star and we were thrilled by her success. The more we could help her succeed on her goals, the better. Unfortunately, our success turned out to be our undoing. Our client sponsor was hired away from the job.

I'll never forget the day we met our sponsor's replacement. The new sponsor invited us to deliver a presentation on our work because he wanted to understand what we were doing, how we were doing it, and why it mattered. Confident in our efforts and armed with examples of our work, we were excited to meet him and show the value we were bringing to the organization. It was important to us that we make a good impression and get started off on the right foot, so we practiced the presentation and brainstormed possible questions that we would have to answer. We were ready.

The meeting ran for about an hour. Three of my colleagues and I shared our team's work and results. We answered his questions, but left the room puzzled. The new sponsor gave us no indication of where we stood. The discussion didn't go poorly, but it didn't go well either. It just kind of went. In our meeting-after-the-meeting, the four of us agreed that it was going to be an interesting road ahead as we collectively yearned for the client sponsor who had left us and the relationship that we had built with her.

The coming weeks and months were tough. Nearly every day, Jamie and I heard concerns from our team about how they were being treated on the client site. Some of their feedback was clearly them just blowing off steam, but much of it was genuinely concerning. On several occasions, we approached the new sponsor and shared our concerns. He appeared to listen and would, at times, agree that he would change how he treated our people. After a few days, however, things always went back to how they were before we talked with him.

Jamie and I were at our wits' end. After much discussion and many sleepless nights, we decided that it was time to fire our biggest client.

We invited our team together and shared our thoughts about ending the relationship. We explained that as painful as it would be, we believed it was time to cut ties and asked each team member to openly share their thoughts on the subject.

Jamie and I listened intently.

It was painfully clear that each team member appreciated that Jamie and I were listening to what they had to say. We didn't try to fix anything; we just listened and absorbed. How do I know that they appreciated our listening? Because of what transpired next.

After everyone shared their concerns, Jamie and I recapped what we heard and reiterated our intent to end the client relationship as what we learned from our team members only fortified our resolve. True, we hated the idea of saying goodbye to 25 percent of our revenue, and we knew we would have to scramble to keep everyone employed, but we were willing to go in that direction because in the end it seemed to be the right decision.

Suddenly, the dialogue shifted. The team began pushing back on us. They argued against firing the client. We were shocked, wondering how they went from complaining about the project sponsor to defending him. A lengthy discussion ensued ending with us collectively agreeing that no matter how much we disliked it, our old sponsor was gone and the new one was here to stay. We agreed that with the new sponsor came problems, but if we looked at things a bit differently, the changes also produced some new opportunities.

Jamie and I left the meeting scratching our heads wondering what had just happened. How did we go from walking in with the intent of firing the client to walking out committed to making it work? How did we go from a team of people who were ready to quit to a team that was ready to fight harder to make it work? In the end, we decided that what happened that day was less about the problems with the client and more about our people feeling heard, having a voice in the discussion, and being empowered to make the decision.

Often in organizations, many people feel that their voice isn't heard, or even welcome. They don't feel like they belong. This phenomenon is not limited to any particular country, industry, or business—it's ubiquitous. This isn't just a concern. It is a tragedy.

The good news is that, regardless of your role, you can be key to helping the voices of others be heard, and to creating a greater sense of belonging and inclusion among team members.

I'm not naive enough to think that everyone has something of significant value to add to every conversation. So, once you allow voices to be heard, you must discern which sentiment should be listened to and acted upon.

Great leaders work to create a culture where everyone gets their say and a chance to be heard. This doesn't mean that every idea is acted upon, but ideas are respectfully heard and considered. Doing that drives performance and feeds our cravings.

DAY 34: FEED CRAVINGS

Today's Thought

Deep down, we all want to be heard. Each of us yearns for our voice to count. We want to be active members of the process, not marginalized actors pushed to the side.

Today's Questions

1. When was the last time that a colleague, boss, or client truly listened to you? How did it feel?

   _____

   _____

2. What is something that you would like to share with your leader? What could you do to facilitate the discussion?

   _____

   _____

Today's Challenge

Find someone who you believe has a genuine concern and a craving to be heard. Ask him to meet today. Listen to the person with the intent of understanding. Don't try to fix the problem; just let the other person be heard. Often, he will be able to fix it without you doing anything but lending a concerned ear.

**DAY
35**

BE A TOUGH ACT TO FOLLOW

once had the opportunity to speak to 120 leaders at the U.S. division of a European-based company. The leaders were embarking on the next phase of a learning journey that they had begun the past summer. My job was to kick off the new phase and to get them excited about the upcoming learning.

Third on the day's agenda, I was comfortably seated in the front of the room, waiting for my time to speak. The company's general manager, who was responsible for all U.S. business, started the day by reviewing current performance, explaining future opportunities, and sharing his commitment to the leadership development efforts. He did an excellent job. I felt confident that, based on his setup, I would be able to deliver on my role.

As the general manager wrapped up his presentation, my attention turned to the next name on the agenda. The person who would speak just before me was Jamie Andrew. Although I had worked with this client for years and knew many of the leaders, I didn't recognize Jamie's name. In a moment, all of that would change.

The general manager introduced Jamie, explaining that he had first heard Jamie speak at a corporate meeting in Switzerland. He shared that Jamie's story was inspirational and he knew that all in the room would be riveted by Jamie's presentation. The crowd provided a warm welcome as the doors to the room opened and Jamie walked to the front.

Over the next thirty minutes, Jamie told the story of climbing with a friend in the Alps some twenty years earlier. Not far from the top of the ascent, the weather turned and the two climbers were forced to make a difficult decision. They either had to descend the treacherous mountain in near-whiteout conditions or wait out the storm at the summit. They elected the latter and managed to dig out a small spot in the ice to hunker down for the night.

One night turned into five. Tragically, Jamie's mate didn't make it through the fifth night. He died on the summit.

The climbers were exposed to −32-degree Fahrenheit (−36-degree Celsius) temperatures, winds of 80 miles per hour (129 kilometers per hour), and relentless snow. On the sixth day, a helicopter managed to drop a rescuer off on the side of the mountain. Heroically, the person scrambled to get to the climbers. He put a harness on Jamie. The helicopter came back around with a ninety-meter line and plucked Jamie from the mountaintop.

Several days later, Jamie found himself in a hospital bed, dealing with the loss of his friend and recovering from having both of his hands and feet amputated. When Jamie finished his story, you could have heard a pin drop. I swallowed hard knowing that I was next to speak. Let's be real. Jamie Andrew is a tough act to follow.

Jamie continued by connecting his experience to what the leaders in the room faced in their roles. He challenged and inspired them. Along the way, he showed me how you can be a tough—yet amazing—act to follow.

Here are three things that you can do to set your successor up for success:

1. DRAW WISDOM FROM YOUR EXPERIENCE AND SHARE IT

There's no doubt that Jamie survived an unbelievable situation. Merely telling his story would have engaged others, but the wisdom from the experience is what was of most value. He was able to share lessons of value to an audience of people who face challenges of their own and will likely never climb in the Alps.

Key leadership lesson: You likely have a few stories of "how we did things back in the day." You may be well practiced at telling them and people might find them entertaining, but they are of little use if you can't help people to connect the experience you had with the challenges they face today. You must make your experiences relevant.

2. CHOOSE THE TOUGH ROAD AND ACHIEVE BIG THINGS OVER TIME

Jamie shared that at one point in his recovery, he set his mind to brushing his own teeth. Up until that point, caretakers had to do it for him. His decision meant that no matter how long it took, he would brush his own teeth. Eventually, he did it. In subsequent days and weeks, he tackled feeding himself and drinking a cup of water on his own. Over time, those tough achievements led him to standing on prosthetic legs, hiking the hills around his home, traveling the world (on his own) to tell his story, and eventually climbing the Matterhorn.

In sharing his goal-setting and accomplishing process, Jamie modeled how to achieve big things. He also challenged the audience to dream of their own professional and personal goals.

Key leadership lesson: Just like Jamie, we face choices every day. Those who choose the tough paths and see them to fruition benefit more from the journey than the destination. Setting and accomplishing small daily goals leads to achieving big things over time. It's through this example that you show others how to win.

3. SURROUND YOURSELF WITH GREAT PEOPLE AND ADD TO THEIR VALUE

Starting with the rescuer who attached the harness to Jamie on the mountaintop, to the helicopter pilot who expertly snatched Jamie from his icy perch, to the doctors, nurses, physical therapists, and other medical professionals, Jamie was surrounded by great people. However, as he explained, the true value of the medical team came to fruition when Jamie started to lead in his own recovery by sharing with them what he needed, helping to orchestrate their efforts, and letting them know how much he appreciated them.

Key leadership lesson: It's important to surround yourself with great people who are highly competent in their roles, but individual performers can only go so far on their own. They need someone to coordinate their efforts, challenge them to improve, and congratulate them when they win!

DAY 35: BE A TOUGH ACT TO FOLLOW

Today's Thought

Drawing wisdom from experiences, choosing the tough road, and surrounding yourself with great people are key ingredients to building a leadership legacy.

Today's Questions

1. When people look back at today, what would you like them to say about you as a leader?

   _____

   _____

2. What are you doing right now to ensure that your answer to the last question becomes a reality?

   _____

   _____

3. What should you start, stop, or continue doing based on your answers to the last two questions?

   _____

   _____

Today's Challenge

Think of a leader from the past whom you truly admire. Imagine you were asked to explain that leader's legacy. Write down three to five items that you would share about how that leader behaved, achieved results, touched lives, and made a difference in the world.

WEEK 5 WRAP-UP

WHAT WILL BE YOUR LEADERSHIP LEGACY?

I magine that it is ten, fifteen, or twenty years in the future. Your colleagues and team members from today have gathered. Their conversation turns to discussing you as a leader. They reminisce about what it was like to work with and for you, what they learned, how they grew, and what they accomplished along the way.

- How do you want to be remembered?
- What do you hope they will say?
- What do you want your legacy to be as a leader?

Use the space on the next page to draft your Leadership Legacy Statement. Reflect on the work you have done over the course of the 5 Week Leadership Challenge—the lessons learned, the questions answered, and the daily challenges completed. Allow that work to assist you as you compose your Leadership Legacy Statement.

If you need help getting started, take a look at the primers on page 194. These are designed to help you to think through some of the keywords others may use in the future when describing you as a leader.

Once you've drafted your Leadership Legacy Statement, share it with a colleague or close associate, ask for advice, and refine your statement as you deem appropriate. Keep the statement visible to yourself. Revisit it often. Allow it to serve as a North Star of sorts as you work to build your leadership legacy.

YOUR LEADERSHIP LEGACY STATEMENT

_____

_____

_____

_____

_____

_____

_____

_____

_____

_____

_____

_____

_____

_____

_____

_____

DO YOU NEED SOME HELP GETTING STARTED
ON YOUR LEADERSHIP LEGACY STATEMENT?

Here are eight leadership skills and behaviors. Under each are words that might be used to describe a great leader who exhibits those skills. Use these words as primers as you draft your Leadership Legacy Statement. Circle the ones that you would like to be part of your legacy and work to incorporate them into your statement.

COMMUNICATE EFFECTIVELY	
Timely	Clear
Transparent	Dynamic
Empathetic	Engaging
Strong listener	Confident
Insightful	Direct

FOSTER INCLUSIVITY	
Value differences	Self-aware
Participative	Considerate
Engagement	Empowering
Open	Connected
Sincere	Courageous

MAKE DECISIONS	
Consistent	Logical
Deliberate	Intuitive
Collaborative	Creative
Problem-oriented	Clever
Resourceful	Decisive

CAST A VISION	
Strategic	Bold
Profound	Nonconformist
Inspiring	Catalyst
Aware	Risk taking
Informed	Optimistic

DEVELOP OTHERS	
Insightful	Helpful
Curious	Concerned
Maximizer	Challenging
Coach	Open
Abundant	Selfless

MANAGE CHANGE	
Flexible	Forward-thinking
Focused	Celebratory
Assertive	Passionate
Reassuring	Embraces ambiguity
Perspective taking	Tenacious

DELIVER RESULTS	
Strong acumen	Savvy
Focused	Meticulous
Goal-oriented	Innovative
Persistent	Accountable
Committed	Competent

LEAD YOURSELF	
Disciplined	Composed
Focused	Balanced
Capable	Grounded
Learner	Intentional
Role Model	Person of integrity

THE JOURNEY CONTINUES

Fellow Leader,

Congratulations, you did it!

You just invested thirty-five days toward becoming the leader you were meant to be. You considered your mindset as a leader and assessed how you choose to approach leading yourself and others. Reflecting on your talents, inner voice, and passion, you defined the purpose behind why you choose to lead. You thought about your priorities, the things you want to accomplish as a leader and with your team, and the plans you will put in place to make them happen. Lastly, you explored how you can inspire a strong performance in yourself and others as you work your way through the daily obstacles on your way to accomplishing what truly matters most.

In the final analysis, people won't remember the specific priorities they are working on today, but they will remember what it felt like to be led by you. I'm confident that the efforts you undertook during the 5 Week Leadership Challenge will go a long way toward building positive and inspiring leadership memories.

Thank you for joining me these last thirty-five days. I wish you the best as you continue on your journey in the weeks, months, and days ahead.

Now, go make it a great day!

Patrick

SCHEDULING YOUR
5 WEEK LEADERSHIP CHALLENGE

Only you can invest in yourself as a leader, and by taking on the 5 Week Leadership Challenge, you're making great strides. Originally I designed the 5 Week Leadership Challenge to provide leaders with a daily dose of learning, seven days per week. As I shared the Challenge with others, I discovered that some people preferred to take it on in four- or five-day sections. Below you'll find schedules to help guide you on whatever path you choose.

Remember, the most important element here is that your plan is realistic and doable.

5 WEEK LEADERSHIP CHALLENGE
7 DAYS PER WEEK CADENCE

SUN	MON	TUE	WED	THU	FRI	SAT
Day 1 Perspective Introduction & Clarify Focus	**Day 2** Engage People	**Day 3** Rethink Failure	**Day 4** Find Guides	**Day 5** Seek Balance	**Day 6** Think Differently	**Day 7** Enjoy the Journey & Weekly Wrap-up
Day 8 Purpose Introduction & Excavate Purpose	**Day 9** Understand Meaning	**Day 10** Uncover Problems	**Day 11** Assess Talent	**Day 12** Explore Passion	**Day 13** Close Doors	**Day 14** Go All In & Weekly Wrap-up
Day 15 Priorities Introduction & Recognize Strategy	**Day 16** Avoid Addictions	**Day 17** Choose Wisely	**Day 18** Be Boring	**Day 19** Ask Customers	**Day 20** Create Momentum	**Day 21** Own the Room & Weekly Wrap-up
Day 22 Plan Introduction & Encourage Ownership	**Day 23** Spur Imagination	**Day 24** Understand Relationships	**Day 25** Remain Open	**Day 26** Let Go	**Day 27** Play to Win	**Day 28** Hit Pause and Engage & Weekly Wrap-up
Day 29 Performance Introduction & Understand Inconsistency	**Day 30** Practice Abundance	**Day 31** Forgo (Some) Happiness	**Day 32** Address Elephants	**Day 33** Unleash Excitement	**Day 34** Feed Cravings	**Day 35** Be a Tough Act to Follow & Weekly Wrap-up

5 WEEK LEADERSHIP CHALLENGE
5 DAYS PER WEEK CADENCE

MON	TUE	WED	THU	FRI
Day 1 Perspective Introduction & Clarify Focus	**Day 2** Engage People	**Day 3** Rethink Failure	**Day 4** Find Guides	**Day 5** Seek Balance
Day 6 Think Differently	**Day 7** Enjoy the Journey & Weekly Wrap-up	**OPEN DAY**	**Day 8** Purpose Introduction & Excavate Purpose	**Day 9** Understand Meaning
Day 10 Uncover Problems	**Day 11** Assess Talent	**Day 12** Explore Passion	**Day 13** Close Doors	**Day 14** Go All In & Weekly Wrap-up
OPEN DAY	**Day 15** Priorities Introduction & Recognize Strategy	**Day 16** Avoid Addictions	**Day 17** Choose Wisely	**Day 18** Be Boring
Day 19 Ask Customers	**Day 20** Create Momentum	**Day 21** Own the Room & Weekly Wrap-up	**OPEN DAY**	**Day 22** Plan Introduction & Encourage Ownership

5 WEEK LEADERSHIP CHALLENGE
5 DAYS PER WEEK CADENCE

MON	TUE	WED	THU	FRI
Day 23 Spur Imagination	**Day 24** Understand Relationships	**Day 25** Remain Open	**Day 26** Let Go	**Day 27** Play to Win
Day 28 Hit Pause and Engage & Weekly Wrap-up	**OPEN DAY**	**Day 29** Performance Introduction & Understand Inconsistency	**Day 30** Practice Abundance	**Day 31** Forgo (Some) Happiness
Day 32 Address Elephants	**Day 33** Unleash Excitement	**Day 34** Feed Cravings	**Day 35** Be a Tough Act to Follow & Weekly Wrap-up	

5-WEEK LEADERSHIP CHALLENGE
4 DAYS PER WEEK CADENCE

MON	TUE	WED	THU	FRI
Day 1 Perspective Introduction & Clarify Focus	**Day 2** Engage People	**Day 3** Rethink Failure	**Day 4** Find Guides	OPEN DAY
Day 5 Seek Balance	**Day 6** Think Differently	**Day 7** Enjoy the Journey & Weekly Wrap-up	**Day 8** Purpose Introduction & Excavate Purpos	OPEN DAY
Day 9 Understand Meaning	**Day 10** Uncover Problems	**Day 11** Assess Talent	**Day 12** Explore Passions	OPEN DAY
Day 13 Close Doors	**Day 14** Go All In & Weekly Wrap-up	**Day 15** Priorities Introduction & Recognize Strategy	**Day 16** Avoid Addictions	OPEN DAY
Day 17 Choose Wisely	**Day 18** Be Boring	**Day 19** Ask Customers	**Day 20** Create Momentum	OPEN DAY

5-WEEK LEADERSHIP CHALLENGE
4 DAYS PER WEEK CADENCE

MON	TUE	WED	THU	FRI
Day 21 Own the Room & Weekly Wrap-up	**Day 22** Plan Introduction & Encourage Ownership	**Day 23** Spur Imagination	**Day 24** Understand Relationships	OPEN DAY
Day 25 Remain Open	**Day 26** Let Go	**Day 26** Play to Win	**Day 28** Hit Pause and Engage & Weekly Wrap-up	OPEN DAY
Day 29 Performance Introduction & Understand Inconsistency	**Day 30** Practice Abundance	**Day 31** Forgo (Some) Happiness	**Day 32** Address Elephants	OPEN DAY
Day 33 Unleash Excitement	**Day 34** Feed Cravings	**Day 35** Be a Tough Act to Follow & Weekly Wrap-up		

APPENDIX B

5 WEEK LEADERSHIP CHALLENGE LEADER'S GUIDE

At its essence, the 5 Week Leadership Challenge is an individual exercise that allows a leader the opportunity to learn, grow, and develop on his or her own. However, the experience can be greatly enhanced when leaders regularly meet to discuss what they are learning and explore how they can apply the challenge concepts across a broader organization.

This guide is designed to help you to facilitate a weekly discussion with leaders as they complete the 5 Week Leadership Challenge. To get the most out of the guide, you should conduct a twenty-minute Challenge Meeting each week after every leader has completed the week's lessons.

Ask participants to come to the meeting prepared to share their general thoughts on the week, as well as their weekly wrap-up assignment.

Meetings should last no more than thirty minutes and should focus on three primary topics.

1. **Review the Week's Theme.** Discuss the main topics covered during the week and the primary outcome from the seven-day effort.

2. **Discuss Individual Takeaways.** Ask each participant to share the two to three key items that they learned that week. These can be items such as:
   - Stories that stood out to them
   - Questions that they found useful
   - Answers that they wrote that gave them more insight into themselves
   - Wrap-up results that they produced

3. **Consider Team Actions.** Discuss as a team how the lessons learned that week can be applied across the entire group and how they can work to hold one another accountable.

INDEX

ABOUT THE AUTHOR

Patrick Leddin has benefited from both hands-on leadership and management experience combined with academic rigor and expertise.

He served as a US Army airborne, infantry, ranger-qualified officer; worked as a project manager at KPMG Consulting; and costarted and ran an Inc. 5000 recognized consulting firm. His speaking engagements and consulting work have allowed him to partner with clients and present to countless audiences in the United States, Canada, China, Malaysia, Singapore, Great Britain, Aruba, Iceland, Germany, Denmark, Belgium, Guam, and many other countries around the world. In addition to his work at Leddin Group, Patrick is an associate professor at Vanderbilt University, where he teaches Negotiation and Leading Business in Times of Crisis. Learn more at LeddinGroup.com.

LEDDINGROUP
THE CHALLENGE IS OVER BUT YOUR LEADERSHIP JOURNEY CONTINUES...
VISIT LEDDINGROUP.COM/LEADER FOR MORE TOOLS AND RESOURCES.